S0-ARL-354

# JOAN EMBERY
## and
# ROBERT VAVRA
# ON
# HORSES

WILLIAM MORROW AND COMPANY, INC.

New York

*We dedicate this book to Duane, not only because it was his idea, but because without his support it would never have been written and photographed.*

Copyright © 1984 by Joan Embery and Robert Vavra

All rights reserved. No part of this book may be reproduced or utilized in any form or by any means, electronic or mechanical, including photocopying, recording or by any information storage and retrieval system, without permission in writing from the Publisher Inquiries should be addressed to Permissions Department, William Morrow and Company, Inc., 105 Madison Ave., New York, N.Y. 10016.

Library of Congress Catalog Card Number: 84-60564

ISBN: 0-688-04070-5

Printed in Spain by Grafos, S. A.
Depósito Legal: B-16.152-1984

First Edition

1 2 3 4 5 6 7 8 9 10

# CONTENTS

# INTRODUCTION

*In the darkness a zebra brayed, followed by the ominous groaning-growling of a camel, and soon joined by the imperious whinnying of a stallion. A human voice rose over the sounds of the animals, "I'll load the zebra, miniature horse, bobcat, and camel. You try to find the macaw. It's seven o'clock and we have to be at Channel Eight in half an hour—it's a live show!" It was the voice of Joan Embery, familiar to millions of television viewers, the Ambassador of Goodwill from the San Diego Zoo, at the beginning of an unusually busy day at the Pillsbury Land and Livestock Company—the horse ranch where she and her husband, Duane, live in Lakeside, California.*

*During the past few years I have had the opportunity to observe men and women—the finest trainers, riders, and breeders—working with horses all over the world. However, though each of these horse people was an expert in his or her own field, I have never met anyone more involved or more skilled in so many different equestrian disciplines than Joan Embery. She rides hunter-jumpers as well as gaited horses and cutting horses, practices dressage as well as driving, and breeds and works draft horses as well as miniatures. She has trained horses to perform with camels, llamas, and other animals.*

*Joan's work and experience with so many exotic wild creatures have given her unique insight into training domestic equines. She has a special touch with horses that I find intriguing. Her ability to express her love for animals has won the respect of millions of American television viewers. She is not only well informed and extremely articulate, but, because animals are her life, she has dealt with situations involving training and behavior that would never occur to the average human being. She has many things to say about equines that I have never before seen in print. The key to the success of Joan Embery on such popular programs as the Merv Griffin show and the Tonight show, where she has appeared more than fifty times, is obviously her love for animals and her talent for showing that love and knowledge. She has a special way with animals which, through her own words in this book, may enrich our own lives and our understanding of horses and ourselves.*

*From a photographer's point of view, Joan Embery is a delight, for she is totally natural and extremely photogenic—the pictures in this book are testimony to that. The days spent taking these photographs were among some of the most pleasant in my memory, not only for the opportunity to be close to equines, both domestic and wild, as well as exotic animals, but also to be with Joan and her husband, Duane, two of the nicest human beings that I have had the good fortune to know.*

—ROBERT VAVRA

# BEGINNINGS

From my earliest childhood I can remember wishing I could have a pony. As I grew older the wish grew, and so did the size of the animal, from pony to horse. Every Christmas I found myself wishing I would be given a real horse. Though I knew the chances were slight that I would receive a live animal, the hope was always in my heart: Maybe, just maybe, I'd be lucky that year.

There was a bowling alley close to our house, and one summer all the kids in our neighborhood signed up to join a bowling league. My mother registered me and my twin sister, Linda, and we went to the bowling alley with everyone else, but I didn't bowl because I wanted to save my money for horseback riding. When my mother learned of this she threatened to stop giving me the money.

While all my friends set their sights on the bowling pins, I set mine more than ever on horses. I continually begged my parents to let me ride, and every now and then I'd get a chance to go out on a trail ride, or my dad, who knew just a little about horses, would take me to the mountains to ride. Finally, when I was about thirteen, my parents, worn down by my determination, began to send me to riding school. I would look forward to those lessons all week long. I would do anything—clean house, scrub floors, do yard work—so that when Saturday came I'd be free to go riding.

Every Friday night I'd iron my riding clothes, polish my boots, and curl my hair. The only time I cared about my appearance was when I was going to the barn. All through junior high school and high school I took group lessons until I was eventually ready for private instruction. Then I began to work with American Saddlebred gaited show horses. I found these animals thrilling to ride—high spirited, high stepping, showy, and refined—"the peacocks of the horse world." However, their spectacularly animated gait is tiring for the horse if he is worked for a long time. When these animals are under saddle, most of the time is spent tuning them for the show ring for which they have been selectively

From her earliest childhood horses meant beauty and romance to Joan.

bred. They aren't really suitable for trail riding. It wasn't until I graduated from high school and began working at the San Diego Zoo that I became involved with showing horses. My job helped to support my growing interest in riding. My parents were helping me through college and, for them, horse shows were a life-style beyond our means.

My first showing experiences were in three-gaited pleasure classes, competing on mounts belonging to the owner of the stable where I took lessons. To pay the entry fees and the cost of hauling to shows, I had to save every penny I could. My first show attire was all secondhand and had to be retailored to fit me. I can remember when I couldn't afford to buy one pair of britches.

Often I shared horses with other riders who, like me, couldn't afford to own their own animals. Sometimes the horse had already been ridden all morning in the junior-division classes. Though I was competitive and usually placed well, I really had to work for it. I didn't have the best horse, I didn't have the best clothes, and I wasn't able to ride every day.

Apart from requiring constant training, gaited horses need special platform shoes, tail sets (harnesses to hold their tails up), and special stalls with tail boards, which prevent them from rubbing their tail sets against the wall. Before long, even though I was doing fairly well in competition, I realized that it was beyond my means to own a really competitive Saddlebred.

I had often watched the jumpers working in the next pasture, and one day I decided to take jumping lessons. I loved it! It was so thrilling to gallop up to a fence and feel the horse collect under me, then spring into the air. Before long I was beginning to show hunters over fences. Hunters are horses of any breed that are judged on their style and manner of going over fences. Through my work with them, I was introduced to the art of dressage and combined training.

With every passing year I grew more and more determined to own a horse of my own. It became my obsession. Nothing was more important. Many of my friends discounted my involvement in social activities with: "All she's interested in are horses." I have to admit that often when I had a date, I'd arrive home late because I had stayed at the stable where I lost all track of time. When darkness came I'd head home and race through the door. My mother would glare at me and continue to entertain my date while I showered and dressed. I spent all my money on horses, and my sister, Linda, spent all hers on clothes. We are not identical twins, and I was forever trying to squeeze into her dresses when I needed something to wear. Naturally that infuriated her, since she was at least one size smaller. Even today, I would rather spend four hundred dollars on a pair of new riding boots than fifty dollars on a pair of lady's dress shoes.

While most people develop an interest in one specific phase of equestrian activities, I found that each area of horsemanship I explored led to another. Pleasure riding led to showing American Saddlebred gaited horses, followed by hunting and jumping, dressage with combined training, driving, horseshoeing, and breeding. Also, I became fascinated with all equines, from miniature horses to draft horses, Przewalskis, zebras, and on and on.

Few animal species are as diversified as equines. From a single wild ancestor, man has been able to develop more than sixty different breeds, each with its own specialty and versatility. Draft horses are immense, powerful work animals, once tremendously important for transportation and agriculture; the small Shetland Pony was trained to work in coal mines; miniature horses became a novelty in royal courts; racehorses were bred for speed; cutting horses for their cow sense. Horses have been developed for color, gait, endurance, and sheerly for beauty. I feel that I could be happy working with any breed of horse and in any kind of activity. The problem with having as many types of horses as I do, and practicing so many varieties of horsemanship without specializing in any single one, is that it's been difficult to keep up with all the different equestrian activities in which I am interested.

My dream of finally owning a horse came true in 1973. When I first spotted Finally, he was only a couple of days old, chestnut in color with legs like stilts, and a tiny dished head marked with a white blaze. He moved so elegantly and seemed so sure of himself, tail carried straight up in the air like a flag, while he ran with his mother. It was love at first sight! My boyfriend at the time, knowing how much I wanted the foal, arranged to buy him for my birthday. I nicknamed him Finally because I finally had a horse of my own!

Waiting until he could be weaned seemed like an eternity, though it was only four months. Finally hadn't been taught anything; he wasn't even accustomed to a halter. When he arrived and we unloaded him from the horse trailer, he tried to run away, pulling the rope so hard that it burned our hands. Until this time, all the animals I had worked were older and trained. From that day on, I spent almost every minute with him when I wasn't at the zoo. When he came down with a bad cold, I slept with him. Once he was halterbroke I took him out for walks everywhere. He seemed more like a dog than a horse. Few colts, I would think, have been handled more than he was.

Finally has always been very people-oriented, probably because of the number of hours I spent with him when he was growing up. Of all the animals in the barn, he is the one horse that will stick his head out of his stall and nicker to me when I come home. If for some reason I had to dispose of my horses, he would be the last one I'd sell. I have never since had enough time to spend that many hours developing such a relationship with any other horse.

When Finally was a year old, like most foals, he went through a very gangly stage: He had long legs, and he started getting white spots on his body. Because he was half Arab and half Quarter Horse, I began to wonder what he was eventually going to look like. I had a chestnut foal, who somewhere in his background must have had gray because he was turning gray. He was going through a color change in which his chestnut and white hairs blended together and produced a sort of rosy cast that eventually became quite beautiful. Since many Arabians mature late, he was also very small as a two-year-old. There was a lot of speculation as to whether he would ever be large enough for me because I am so tall. I was delighted on his fourth birthday, when he stood 15.3 hands high.

Since I couldn't ride Finally when he was young, and I was working with a man at the zoo who had circus horses, I learned from him how to train my colt for Liberty work. Finally learned to do the Spanish walk, march, bow, rear, nod his head *yes* and shake it *no*, and come when he was called. He looked forward to his training sessions and learned quickly. Even today, at the age of ten, he still loves to perform.

Since Finally could not be ridden until he was at least two, I continued to ride other horses, and it was then that I acquired Eagle. A trainer at the zoo told me about a gray Thoroughbred he had bought from a racing stable. He had planned on doing some dressage training with his new horse, but found he didn't really have enough time; so we worked out a plan together. Since I wanted a horse to ride, I agreed to take Eagle and train him as a hunter, and if the horse was sold, I would receive a percentage of the sale. Steel gray with beautiful dapples, and very showy, Eagle had raced for five years, was high strung, athletic, and was the most challenging horse I had ever worked. My first ride out on a trail with him was down a graded dirt roadway that was being prepared for a major highway. Things went well until, about five miles from the stable, we turned for home. It was then that Eagle decided to run, and nothing I could do would stop him. I had a simple snaffle in his mouth, and he just took hold of the bit and headed for the finish. I got my first taste of what it must be like to be a jockey. It was terrifying; the wind whipped my ears as I thought what could happen if he stumbled on that rough road. The harder I pulled on the reins, the stronger he pulled. I began to pump him back by alternately pulling and releasing the reins, as my sister raced to catch up with me. Finally, I was able to ease him back gradually. When my sister caught up and helped to slow us down, I could then understand the role of pony horses on the track. We must have covered three to four miles in a matter of minutes. Once Eagle was under control, my concern turned to his legs. I wondered if he had damaged them. Back at the stable I carefully rubbed down his legs and wrapped them.

The next day I was relieved to find him in good condition; however, it was quite a while before I rode him out on the trail again. It took considerable effort to overcome his past experience on the track. Though he was handsome and a real athlete, he was also headstrong and temperamental. After some months of working Eagle over fences, I finally decided to put him on the market, but since we asked a pretty good price, I didn't expect an immediate sale. However, the second prospective buyer who came to the stable watched Eagle work and said, ''I'll take him!'' I was shocked. Suddenly I realized how attached I'd grown to that stubborn gray horse, and, after some serious thinking, I decided to buy him myself. Instead of making a commission, I ended up raiding my savings account. From that point on I put most of my funds, outside of living expenses, into my horses.

# THE ZOO

Joan has been the San Diego Zoo Ambassador of Goodwill for fourteen years.

When I entered college I was primarily interested in equine medicine. The veterinary schools with whom I corresponded replied that I needed to have some practical experience in order to demonstrate that I had an understanding of working with animals. It was then that I applied to every veterinary hospital in San Diego, as well as at Sea World and the zoo. About nine months passed before I received my first call from the zoo. Later, I learned that for the approximately one thousand jobs available at the zoo, there are ten thousand applications on file, and of all the zoo employees, only about two hundred actually work with animals. Most San Diego Zoo applicants would take any job available just to be able to be part of what is considered the world's finest animal park. The majority of new zoo employees who are fortunate enough to be hired to work with animals start ''on call.''

When I began at the zoo, I had to wait by the phone every day to see whether I would be called in to work. Though my supervisors did try to arrange my schedule around my college classes, I never left the house before ten A.M. or until I

had heard if I was going to be needed at the zoo. Sometimes I worked every day and sometimes I went for weeks at a time without being called. As an attendant at the Children's Zoo, I was an intermediary between the public and the animals: answering questions, cleaning cages, feeding, and working with young wild animals. There, I had the opportunity to work with them before they became too tough to handle

It was a wonderful starting point because I was able to build up my confidence while relating on a one-to-one basis with all types of creatures: tapirs, llamas, elephants, lions, tigers, apes. Although my primary interest at the time was horses, I was fascinated with the diversity of zoo inhabitants. My favorite animals have always been wild equines and elephants—elephants, primarily because of their intelligence and size. My knowledge of horses helped tremendously in training elephants, who I found to be even brighter than I had expected. It was easy to relate my work with them to that of equines, since both are large animals, and both attempt to attain dominance in relationships within their own species and with humans, which means that the animal's will often has to be overridden in order to control it. I had an advantage over many of the new employees at the zoo who had not worked with horses. The girls without experience with large animals didn't want to work with elephants because they got pushed around by them. They preferred cats, apes, or hooved animals. I felt fairly comfortable with a baby elephant, which was about the size of a horse and not much more difficult to work, as long as I was able to impose my will. During this time, even though I was working at the zoo, I was also riding, training, and showing horses. The zoo job provided me with an income to pursue my horse interests.

Since I started at the zoo at the bottom of the totem pole as an "on call" employee, I got all the lesser jobs: cleaning out the incubator, scrubbing floors, and working with "less interesting" animals.

After two years in that position, I was finally promoted to regular hours. I was also able to work with even more animals as I advanced in seniority. Some of that time I spent in the nursery, which was a very desirable position. Only girls who had been employed at the Children's Zoo for quite a while were given that opportunity. The job required more training because the animals sometimes needed veterinary assistance or special care. Being part of the nursery was interesting, yet as much fun as it was, working with larger animals was what I enjoyed most. Taking care of small, fragile creatures that sometimes were frail and near death was not as much fun as training elephants. In fact, I was so happy with the elephants that I began spending a lot of off-duty hours with them.

When the zoo created the position of Goodwill Ambassador, out of hundreds of applicants they picked a professional model. However, the next time the Goodwill Ambassador position was vacant, with even more applicants, it was decided to select someone with a better understanding of animals, which caused the zoo to start looking within their own organization. Having had two years experience in the Children's Zoo, I had an advantage over the other applicants. Also, I had taken part in several television shows, assisting backstage with animals. At that time, however, I had only appeared once or twice on camera, and didn't really feel comfortable on television. That took quite a while. Due to my lack of experience as a public speaker, when I was given the job, I was at the same time excited and frightened by the overwhelming responsibility of representing the zoo. I found myself in a sink-or-swim situation with a lot of learning to do. The Goodwill Ambassador position would provide the chance to get more involved with handling and training animals. It offered the opportunity to work with trainers and keepers, which I hadn't been able to do because in those days there weren't any female keepers or trainers.

Obviously, I do not have the qualities needed for modeling for television or for photography. I am five foot ten inches and weigh 150–160 pounds, depending on how busy I am, how hard I work, and how much I eat. I'm just a large person. The first time I was not self-conscious about my size was when I started working with the larger animals at the zoo, and I could say to myself, "Hey, don't knock it because you're large. If you weren't, you wouldn't be able to get through that show, or move a hundred-pound bale of hay. You wouldn't have been able to control the elephant if you hadn't the size and strength to do so." So I learned to accept my size and to realize that in many ways it is an asset. However, I must admit that even today I sometimes feel frustrated by the big muscles I have developed, and by the fact that I do not have the picture-perfect model size. When I work in television, I look at women who are there for their beauty, and I feel a little awkward. However, I realize that whatever appeal I may have is not based on my looks, but on my ability to work with and handle animals, some of which are dangerously large. The bottom line, of course, is the fact that my job is to show animals, and how I look is secondary.

One of the most frustrating things about being involved in so many diverse aspects of horsemanship—with all the different breeds and equestrian activities—is that in a lifetime a person can't hope to gain but a fraction of the expertise he or she would like to have in any one field. I could name a trainer in each specific area who probably knows as much as there is to know about that particular area, but they devote all their time to that one specialty. Within the zoo we have a curator of birds, a curator of reptiles, a curator of mammals, and a primatologist, a behavioralist, and other research people divided into all different areas of the medical fields. Because I represent the zoo in general, I have to know a little bit of everything. This can be somewhat overwhelming and frustrating at times, because the public expects me to know everything. If I don't know the answer to a particular question, I say so and go to find the answer.

Fortunately, my work with elephants and other exotic animals, along with the opportunity to study their natural behavior, has given me more insight into my work with horses. On a day-to-day basis it is interesting to observe the reactions of horses to external things. The flight distance of creatures living free is much greater, their reaction time is faster, and they are more easily threatened. If you have worked with zebras, Przewalskis, and other wild animals, you become amazed about what you can do with a domestic horse and get away with. You would never be able to accomplish these things with a Przewalski or zebra. You could—without success—spend your whole life trying to teach them to do the things for which our horses have been bred selectively. Working with wildlife offers an understanding of the true nature of the domestic horse.

# EVOLUTION

When I first became interested in horses, I was fascinated to learn that their history, traced through fossil remains, began millions of years before the history of man. The first horse appeared more than 50 million years ago, and since then more than 250 different types of horses have lived on earth.

The first ancestor of my horse Finally was Eohippus (meaning *dawn horse*) a small animal slightly larger than a fox, about twelve inches tall, with four toes on the front feet and three toes on the hind feet, and with slender legs, a short neck, and even teeth. Well adapted to traveling in and feeding upon the vegetation of swamplands, the descendants of Eohippus gradually grew in size and changed in form, evolving into a three-toed animal known as Mesohippus, which was approximately two feet high. Further changes continued, transforming the animal from an inhabitant of the swamp to a creature capable of surviving in the forest and, finally, to one adapted to the prairie.

As the animal grew taller, its teeth became longer, stronger, and more roughened to suit the gradual changes to grazing on the prairie. The cannon bones—metacarpals and metatarsals—lengthened; the middle toe (or third toe) grew longer and stronger, developing into a hoof; and the other toes (second and fourth) gradually disappeared, except for vestiges, the slender bones known as splints, under the skin. The transformation in length and structure of the foot made for greater speed over prairie-type terrain, thus allowing the animal to range and feed farther and farther from water, while providing it with greater safety in its struggle to survive. Horses are marvelous examples of the slow adaptation of animal life to changing conditions in environment, climate, food, and soil.

By the time America was discovered, horses had disappeared from the New World. Why horses perished on the American continent, only a few thousand years before Columbus discovered America, is still one of the unexplained mysteries of evolution. Their disappearance was so complete and sudden, many scientists believe that it must have been caused by some contagious disease or fatal parasite. Others feel that perhaps it was due to multiple causes, including (1) climatic changes, (2) competition for food and space, and/or (3) failure to adapt. Regardless of why horses disappeared, conditions in America were favorable for them when they were brought from Europe by the Spanish conquistadores less than five hundred years ago. These animals were the offshoot of ancestral stock, improved and refined by thousands of years of domestication and use by mankind.

Zebras, horses, and asses all belong to the family Equidae. Equids are a part of the order Perissodactyla—odd-toed hooved mammals—of which there are three living families: horses, tapirs, and rhinos. Like both of their

Wild asses still inhabit certain parts of the world. Here, Joan is shown with a burro and an Andean condor, both of which are found in South America.

heavy-bodied relatives, equines in their truly wild form are relatively rare in the world today, and many are faced with extinction. Already extinct are the tarpan, quagga, Burchell's zebra, and Syrian wild ass. Conservation studies of endangered or threatened equine species provide the following rough estimates for the total numbers now in existence: the Przewalski's horse—500, Cape mountain zebra—200, Hartmann's mountain zebra—5,000, Grévy's zebra—15,000, Somali wild ass—3,000, Indian wild ass (khur)—300, Mongolian wild ass (kulan)—7,000, Persian wild ass (onager)—500, and Tibetan wild ass (kiang)—3,000. Today, wild horses are found only in Africa, Asia, and in zoos. The three types of true wild horses with which I have worked are onagers, Przewalski's horses, and zebras.

# PRZEWALSKI

The Przewalski horse from Mongolia and China is the only true wild horse that exists today. Primitive drawings on cave walls in southern France and northern Spain show little change in their appearance over more than fifteen thousand years. The Przewalski has a short, stiff mane that stands erect (like the wild ass and the zebra), no forelock, short hair at the base of the tail, and a dorsal stripe down the back. In general, the Mongolian wild horse is smaller than a domestic horse, thirteen to fourteen hands, but has a larger, blockier head. With light-colored hair around the eyes and muzzle, the rest of the body is various shades of reddish brown.

The existence of these horses was officially documented and recorded in 1881, when Colonel Nikolai Przewalski, a Polish officer in the Imperial Russian Army, who had explored the wastelands of northern China, sent the skin and skull of an unknown wild horse to the Soviet Academy of Sciences in Leningrad, where it was stuffed and still stands. That specimen convinced zoologists of the presence of a species considered extinct, along with the other equine prototype, the tarpan.

Coupled with the spread of man and his domestic animals into previously unoccupied areas, the unfortunate decline of the Przewalski horse dates from the acquisition of modern firearms by Chinese and Mongolian hunters. With competition for grazing and water, only the forbidding terrain north of Tibet and in Mongolia offered sanctuary.

The first Przewalski horses were captured for zoos by using relays of riders on fresh horses that would chase a herd until the foals dropped from exhaustion. Domestic nursemares then accompanied the young Przewalskis to Europe. The mortality rate was high, but more than fifty of these Mongolian wild horses did survive and reached collections in Russia, Germany, and England. The United States got its first specimens when the Bronx Zoo imported a pair in 1902.

Although breeding went well for many years, the captive herds diminished, so that by the mid-1950s only four animals existed in North America, with no viable offspring. Many of the European collections were allowed to die out or

Although this Przewalski stallion that Joan feeds looks tame, a year earlier he had broken the arm of a keeper.

were killed by bombs during World War II. By that time the gene pool was in a perilous state. Fortunately, while groups of animals in the Western world were on the decline, Munich and Prague maintained sizable herds, and it is from these collections that the North American bloodlines were strengthened. In 1956, the Catskill Game Farm imported two stallions and four mares from Munich, which in 1966 provided the San Diego Zoo with two mares and one stallion.

Since not a single animal has been sighted in the wild since 1968, the Przewalski horse's history in captivity has been the key to its survival. If any exist in Mongolia or China, it is unlikely that they do so in numbers large enough to prevent extinction.

All the Przewalski horses now in captivity trace their ancestry to twelve individuals—eleven wild specimens brought into Europe around 1900, and one additional animal, Orlitza, who was captured in 1947. Today, there are five hundred of these rare Mongolian horses in major zoos around the world (about ninety in the United States), with the world pedigree book kept at the Halle-Prague Zoo. The San Diego Zoo has recorded nine Przewalski births, and the Wild Animal Park, twenty-seven births. Foals are named according to a system that reflects their breeding: Their names begin with the first two letters of their mother's name. For example, the names of all horses descended from Bonnette begin with the letters *Bo*.

Though the Przewalski is seemingly safe through captive breeding programs, it faces yet another threat—inbreeding. In addition to the dangerous limited foundation stock, many institutions in the past have mated only members of their own small herds, using the same sire for years without any thought to the long-range consequences. In an effort to spread the gene pool, parks now work together to attain new bloodlines by exchanging animals with the greatest genetic distance. These combinations are carefully worked out by a geneticist and a computer. The program happily led to a trade of horses between the San Diego Zoo and Askaniya Nova, Ukraine, the Russian breeding farm. This was the first exchange of its kind.

My good luck in having the chance to work with a Przewalski was the result of an unfortunate accident. One night after a filly foal was born at the Wild Animal Park, it was found with a broken leg; presumably it had been stepped on by another horse. Rather than destroy the foal, whose name was Bosaga, the zoo decided to attempt to set the bone, utilizing a new plating procedure. The operation was performed at the zoo hospital by Dr. Jane Meier and Dr. Phil Robinson. Unlike human patients who can be told to stay in bed or use crutches, most animals immediately try to use an injured limb, which they find difficult to move in a heavy plaster cast. Bone plating—screwing the broken ends of a bone to a metal plate to bring them together—a technique practiced in human medicine for many years, is being used with increasing frequency in animal medicine. In Bosaga's case, a stainless steel plate and five screws were used to stabilize the fracture. The operation was successful, and Bosaga, because of the frequent treatment she required, was raised in the Care Center, where the strong but light fiberglass cast used on her leg could be replaced every seven to ten days. When she was ready to leave the Care Center she was given to our horse show with the understanding that as soon as she reached maturity, because she was so rare and valuable as a breeding animal, she would be shipped to another zoo.

Through the horse show we were able to share Bosaga with the public and demonstrate her uniqueness. A year later when we X-rayed her leg, it was difficult to look at the film and determine which leg had been broken because the bone had healed so well. Although Bosaga looked like a horse and had similar behavior, she was very much a wild animal. When she was young she would accept most people, but as she grew older she became more selective. She knew everybody in the horse show; she had likes and dislikes. There were certain people of whom she would be more tolerant than others. If a veterinarian or an unfamiliar keeper came too close, she would immediately pin her ears, squeal, and kick at him. The degree to which she could identify each human was amazing. She didn't seem to like people who wore uniforms. The behavior that we saw developing as she matured was probably the herd instinct. The people she worked with every day were part of her group, or herd. Strangers she didn't know were not part of her band, and were not acceptable.

First, we halterbroke Bosaga so that we could lead her out in front of the public. Though she was then trained to get up on a tub and stand there, we never really tried to teach her tricks because she was our example of how the horse show related to the Wild Animal Park. Bosaga justified the presence of domestic equines at the park. She was used as an educational tool, an example of the raw, simple material from which man has created dozens of breeds of horses, each with its own special physical appearance and performance aptitude. To train her as a domestic horse would have been to minimize her role as the wild creature she was.

Bosaga's presence in the show gave people an appreciation for free-living equines. It definitely helped convince our audiences that horses should be able to exist as wild animals, although what was once considered wild is rapidly changing. Unfortunately, in order to keep areas wild, they must be managed. There is a desperate need to relate to people who have no feel for nature, conservation, and the value of wild animals. In the wild, because of the animal's flight distance, a person could never get close to a Przewalski; it would run at the first hint of danger. At the park's Mongolian horse enclosure, visitors can see the animals, but still at a distance. In the show they could see Bosaga

The Przewalski horse is the only true wild horse and is probably now extinct in its natural habitat, Mongolia.

being handled by humans, and so it was easier for the public to relate to her. Visitors would walk along the row of horses used in the show, patting them all. We had to warn them continually that when they got to Bosaga's stall she might try to kick them.

Our Przewalski mare's wild temperament indicated that attempts at training her would have been not only difficult but limited. Being able to present Bosaga a few feet away from the show spectators, while pointing out all her unique features and behavioral differences, helped people to become interested in what she was, why she was special, and why we should try to save her breed.

Mankind has an unrepayable debt to wild equines, and yet most humans are unconcernedly watching them being pushed toward extinction. The fate of these animals relates to how humans perceive them and whether we are willing to make an effort to allow them to prosper rather than become extinct. Horses gave man mobility. In part, they have helped carry us to where we are today. Used in agriculture, to transport America westward, to deliver mail, for battle— they were important to every aspect of progress.

How unfortunate it is that man perceives himself as the supreme being with the power to decide which species should live and which should die. Humans and animals were all put on this earth as equals. Why then should man now decide irresponsibly the fate of other species that seem of no material use to him? Can we not co-exist? Working with wildlife, I find it frightening to see just how many species of animals are extinct and how many species are close to extinction. We may soon find that we have pushed things too far, and it will be too late to bring back to life creatures we blindly assumed did not serve a function.

The training hours spent with Bosaga, the Przewalski mare, were unique. I found in dealing with her that she became more tolerant in time, more accepting of being handled and controlled. I always had the feeling that whatever I accomplished with her was possible because she had allowed me to do what I did, and not because I had imposed my will on her. It would have been difficult to force her to do anything, because Przewalskis don't accept discipline the way domestic horses do. You can punish a Thoroughbred, for example, when it misbehaves, but if you discipline a wild equine, it retaliates or fights you, and can become aggressive and dangerous. If Bosaga didn't want to lead, often I simply waited and stood my ground and hoped that she would give in, because to discipline her might have created an even greater conflict—this seemed to be true for all the wild equines with whom I have dealt. They have to be convinced that what you want them to do is easier than resisting, that they won't be hurt by it—mutual trust is absolutely an essential factor in working with them.

Bosaga was in the show about three years, until she reached maturity, when it was decided that because of the small number of captive/living Przewalski's horses, she should then be sent to a breeding group. Even though from the moment she was entrusted to me I knew that this would happen eventually, when the time came it was very difficult for me to give her up. We had an unusual relationship, one that would end once she became part of a herd and was no longer handled. My husband, Duane, and I transported her by trailer to the Denver Zoo; and it grew increasingly more difficult as we went farther and farther from San Diego, knowing that we didn't have much more time left with her.

We hauled Bosaga in a regular two-horse trailer, and there the advantage of having trained her was very apparent and useful. We could walk her into the trailer, tie her up, walk in and out of the trailer, and handle her. She never resisted, but accepted everything that had to do with the trip. She looked forward to the times we would stop and go back to talk to and feed her. People would always ask what we had in the trailer, and when we would let them peek in, their response was usually, ''What a good-looking mule you've got there.'' I found this highly amusing. Years before, it had seemed like a miracle when she was placed in my care, and now, away from the Animal Park, people reacted to her as if she were something they saw every day. When I would explain that she was a very rare endangered horse from the Mongolian steppes, people would look at me as if they were thinking, ''Sure, lady, what type of fish story is this?'' Then, as I'd tell them a little more about her and point out her mane, tail, and color, shape of head, and markings, they'd become more interested and realize that what I was saying was true.

Late at night when we arrived at the Denver Zoo, everyone who was anxiously awaiting Bosaga was amazed by her temperament. Their only previous contact with Przewalskis had been with wild ones and they were fascinated to see that she was manageable. She was given a big stall that was heated and bedded, and it was nice to know that she was in good hands. But it was still difficult when I took that halter off, knowing that she'd never wear one again. However, it was also exciting to realize that she was going to become a broodmare and produce foals, and to think that we'd been a part of her past as well as her future, and that of all Przewalskis.

Months later I was thrilled to learn that Bosaga had been bred and was pregnant, and that our handling of her had not affected her productivity in any way. It delighted me to remember that she had been introduced to thousands of people at the Wild Animal Park, as well as on national television. She was certainly the first live Przewalski to ever appear on a television show watched by thirty million people. I know I must have pointed out to Johnny Carson and the *Tonight* show audience that although Bosaga might look almost like a normal horse, Johnny should keep his distance and remember she was definitely a wild animal who barely trusted those of us who were familiar to her. We then gave her treats of milk or grain so that she would be more tolerant of Johnny and the other people on the show. If a stranger with food entered her territory, he was much more likely to be accepted than if he didn't have anything to offer her.

When Bosaga did give birth, I was distressed to hear that she had prolapsed her uterus and was found having foaled with it dragging on the ground. Not only was her survival in question, but it was doubtful that she could ever be bred again. A year passed, and last September at the National Zoo Conference I was overjoyed to learn that she had successfully foaled, which was really amazing considering her condition and what she'd been through. When her uterus prolapsed they operated on her and put it back in place, which luckily didn't seem to have any effect on her next foal, a colt born in 1983.

When wild horses are in captivity they become accustomed to being handled, and when things are going normally it is not unusual for a trainer or keeper to let his or her guard down. With many wild animals it is easy to develop a false sense of security, thinking, ''I have control, I do this every day,'' until something happens to cause the animals to show their true colors. This may come in the form of aggressiveness, or threat.

Rich Massena, a head keeper who works with the Przewalski horses, among other animals at the Wild Animal Park, could easily have lost his life when he was attacked by a stallion that had recently arrived at the park from England. While I was being photographed feeding this same horse a carrot, Rich told Robert Vavra and me of his experience:

On March twenty-eighth at seven A.M. I received a call from some of my fellow keepers that one of the Przewalskis had foaled and the foal seemed unable to get out of a ravine. I went down into the ravine to remove the foal, while the other keepers kept the stallion and the mare from attacking. This worked out fine until I reached the top of the canyon where it was a little flatter and we tried to reintroduce the foal by laying it down and showing it to the mother. The mare was attempting to get back to the foal, at which time the stallion attacked and forced us into our trucks. He then grabbed the foal by the base of the mane and threw it high into the air. With our two trucks we forced him away from the foal and surrounded it. I leaped out of the truck and grabbed the foal and then jumped back into the open truck bed, telling my coworker that we'd better get out of there, as the foal was sure to be injured. We arrived at the far end of the exhibit with the stallion lunging and charging, the whole time trying to get into the back of the truck where I was. The

The San Diego Wild Animal Park has had much success in breeding Przewalskis.

foal was vocalizing, which obviously was attracting the stallion and making him more excited.

When we arrived at the gate we realized that there was no way either my fellow keeper or I could get out of the truck to open it without being attacked by the stallion, who was still trying to jump into the back of the truck. In this particular truck there was a toolbox, and I was attempting to push the foal under it while at the same time trying to keep an eye on the angry stallion. I was shoving the foal with my right arm and at one point swung at the stallion with my left arm, at which time he grabbed it, lifted me out of the truck and shook me back and forth a couple of times. I felt my arm break, and then he slipped and started falling backward and let go of me, which probably saved me from being lifted out of the truck and thrown onto the ground. A couple of seconds later a third keeper arrived in another truck and drove the stallion off. We were able to get out of the exhibit and turn the foal over to another truck, which rushed it to the Care Center where it later died. I was taken to the hospital and found that both bones in my left arm were broken.

When we asked Rich how the accident affected his work, he replied,

I think it makes you more cautious—not that we're not cautious out here at the park—all of the keepers know you can get hurt at any time. However, the reality of an accident happening is brought home quite dramatically when you receive an injury like mine. I wasn't really intimidated about coming back into the Przewalski's exhibit after having my arm broken, but I do find myself thinking more about the stallion and his potential. You know what his potential is, but you don't expect him to react like that.

When accidents like Rich's occur, you see just how powerful these animals can be, and how potentially dangerous they are. When working with them it should be remembered that they are really just allowing a human to deal with them. If they actually wanted to, they could seriously injure any of us.

I think that when it comes to training wild horses, or most animals, the key to success is knowing exactly how far you can push them and how much reward or discipline is necessary to achieve the desired behavior. The combination of reward and punishment, and knowing where to draw the line between the two, is the key to successful training. That line is different for every animal. A certain amount of discipline or control is necessary to be able to deal with any horse, but on the other hand, accomplishment is the result of a positive relationship, which is formed by the trust between animal and trainer.

Like Rich, my most serious injury working with animals was a broken arm, which was received from a horse while preparing for a photograph in this book. I have been bitten, scratched, kicked, butted—everything that an animal can do I've experienced in one way or another. However, during the years, as Rich said, I think that people who work with animals develop a confidence in what they are doing, and when an accident happens we become a little more cautious. However, confidence on the trainer's part must always be shown, whether or not he or she has had an accident.

It is almost certain that if a person is truly frightened, an animal senses that fear. Body language, the way a person moves, hesitantly or securely, the tone of voice—nervousness is transmitted immediately by voice—are all of extreme importance in dealing with animals. If a person is frightened of an animal, there is little chance of controlling it. A trainer can't be frightened, but he or she had darn well better have respect for the animal. If respect for an animal's potential danger is ignored, the chances are that the trainer is going to go too far, or going to do something stupid, which could result in hurting himself, another person, or the animal. It is hard to determine the way animals feel unless much time is spent observing them, being around them, trying to learn to think the way they do, and attempting to perceive how they're going to react before they do. Then, the trainer can only hope that his interpretation has been correct.

Horses can determine dominance and subordinance by sniffing each other. A certain amount of trembling also goes on when a horse is afraid. Humans communicate primarily by spoken language and rely very much on it, whereas animals perceive things more by body language, smell, and sight. People can hide their emotions, but animals are pretty upfront about them. One good example of how people, judging from their own human experience, misread animal body language, is illustrated by the chimp that smiles, appearing to give the impression it is happy. Smiling among primates is really a threat gesture. Horses also appear to smile—"flehmen"—when in reality they are not, by equine interpretation, doing that at all.

# ZEBRAS

Being nuts over horses, I had always been fascinated by zebras—but from a distance. According to most of the keepers I had talked with, they were unapproachable. I was told they would kick my teeth out, and they couldn't be trained. Still, I was sure there must be a way somehow. One day when I was working at the Wild Animal Park, I saw a new zebra foal in the Care Center. She had become ill after her birth and had been taken there for treatment. Since a zebra mare will not allow her foal to be handled, it became necessary to hand raise this foal. When she was in good health, I badgered the curator to let me try my hand at raising her.

Zelda, as she was named, was delivered to the park's back gate in a large wooden crate. We put it in our pickup truck, tied it securely, and headed for the ranch. I couldn't wait to see her, touch her, and give her her milk formula. To my surprise, once she was settled in her stall and I entered it, I was promptly kicked right back out again. Zelda was not one to make friends quickly I found out. She was on guard with strangers. It took three of us to get a halter on her, and she was only two months old.

After days of bottle-feeding and befriending Zelda, we decided to try to take her out of the stall on a lead. However, she was so difficult to control that we had to use two ten-foot lead ropes to steady her, which prevented her from wheeling and kicking either of us. This system had to be used until we eventually were able to drop one of the leads when she became more accustomed to her outings. She was already tremendously powerful, and growing larger and stronger every day. Because of predators such as lions, hyenas, hunting dogs, and leopards, zebra foals must be able to get to their feet and run soon after birth. When a zebra cannot outrun a predator, it will stand its ground and kick or bite. It is capable of breaking the skull of a full-grown lion. Because Zelda was so accurate with her hooves, we realized we'd better move fast with her training program while we still had a size advantage.

Zelda was trained to tie by tying her to an inner tube hung in her stall, which we then moved to a tie rack. Temperamental as she was, she loved company and resented being tied at first, especially when we moved out of sight. She

Letty, the Hartmann's zebra, and Zelda, the Grévy's zebra, were both bottle raised by Joan.

Showing their flight distance, a herd of Hartmann's zebras scatter behind Joan at the San Diego Wild Animal Park.

would vocalize with a honking sound until she could see us. In the wild, excited zebras pursued at night by predators use their barking call to maintain contact with herd members. Learning to tie helped teach her to lead, because she found she could pull with all her might without being able to get anywhere. The inner tube protected her neck with a quick jerk, acting as a shock absorber. It was amusing to watch her play tug-of-war. She wasn't about to give in at first, then she would slacken momentarily, only to pull back again in defiance. It was a tough lesson to learn, but with that major step mastered, we moved on to loading her into a horse trailer. For us to use her in promotions and on television, she had to be willing to be hauled. Again, she was reluctant at first. As an extra enticement we used her bottle of milk, which she dearly loved, as a bribe. I remember walking up behind her to coax her in as Duane led her up to the trailer. She kicked out, so to try and make her move forward I started to pick up a stick with which to touch her hindquarters. But as I was doing this, Zelda was so aware of everything around her that she saw my hand move and managed to precisely kick the stick out of my hand. With perseverance and encouragement we were finally able to load her.

Each day was a little easier until Zelda finally became comfortable about being in the trailer. Next, we decided it was time to take her for a ride. Duane kept her company while I drove. All went well, and we let her ride alone on the next trip. When we got out of the truck, she called to us as if to say, "Where are you going? Can I come out now? Don't leave me here alone."

Wherever we took Zelda she always drew a lot of attention with her huge ears and vivid stripes. We learned that although zebras are equines, they are definitely a "horse of a different color." They are wild animals. They are not as calm and responsive as domestic breeds. Through selective breeding, man seeks and enforces "workable temperament" in domestic stock. Nature, on the other hand, and also by the use of selective breeding—survival of the fittest—creates animals that to us are unworkable and difficult. Zebras do not accept discipline and restraint as do domestic equines. I remember coming home late one night after a trip to a Los Angeles television show. As I entered the back of the trailer to remove Zelda, she kicked at me. I slapped her on the rump to discourage her bad behavior and

24

before I knew what had happened, I was kicked out of the back of the truck and landed on the tailgate. My legs were black and blue for weeks.

Zebras do not always warm up to strangers. Maybe it's the herd instinct, or just a general wariness. They definitely know who's who. When Zelda meets strangers, she is inclined to swing her hindquarters into the threat or ready position. She may not even kick, but she is in a position to do so if she wants. She reacts the same way to stray dogs, or anything she's not sure of. To encourage her to accept visitors, we let them give her a bottle of milk, which she is willing to follow almost anywhere. On her fussy days she will drink like mad, but grunt when they touch her as if to say, "You can feed me but don't touch."

The year after we acquired Zelda, we were offered a second zebra from the Wild Animal Park's Care Center—a Hartmann's mountain filly that was almost four months old. She had been removed from the field when she was rejected by her mother, who had been immobilized for hoof trimming. Native to rough, mountainous terrain, their rapid-growing hooves are worn down by rocks. In captivity their hooves frequently grow excessively long and must be trimmed. Since a zebra will not stand still to have its hooves trimmed, it must be immobilized. This procedure, which is rapid, usually has no ill effect on the animal. For some unknown reason, this foal's mother, once she had regained consciousness, would not accept her baby. The filly was a healthy foal, unlike most of the other young animal arrivals who were at the Care Center because of ill health, and she soon became a favorite of many of the attendants working there. Since she was growing rapidly, I was asked if I would like to continue raising Letty, as she had been named, at the ranch.

When it was decided to move Letty from the park to the ranch in a standard two-horse trailer, we attempted at first to coax her into it. When that didn't work, we resorted to pushing. Finally, we had to carry her inside. Once the doors closed she was obviously near panic, ready to try and find any way to escape. Since there was an open space between the trailer roof and the top of the closed doors, we were worried she might try to jump out. Fortunately, the park staff found a sheet of plywood, which they cut and placed across the open space. To calm our precious cargo, Duane rode in the trailer with Letty as I drove home cautiously. It seemed to take forever to cover the twenty-five miles of winding mountain roads to our ranch. With each turn I worried, not only about Letty, but that Duane could also be hurt if she became too excited. I would call back to him at each stop we made. It was such a relief when we pulled into the ranch. And it was almost unbelievable to me that after all those years of wanting the chance to work with one zebra, I now had two.

Zelda and Letty, besides being different species, were different in many respects. Zelda was quick to kick but

didn't attempt to bite, while Letty never threatened to kick but was inclined to use her teeth on anything in reach, including people. Letty seemed to like everyone and appreciate attention, while Zelda continued to narrow the field of those she would accept. Zelda was reluctant to have her legs handled, always wanting to be in control. Letty was trained more easily to pick up her feet. We worked extra hard to train her to pick up her feet, knowing they would need to be trimmed more often. Zelda, like all Grévy's zebras, has broad hooves, while Letty, like all Hartmann's, has long, narrow hooves for sure footing in rocky terrain. To this day, I still trim her feet every four to six weeks, while Zelda's have never needed to be trimmed at all.

In the spring of 1983, I was asked to develop a show for the zoo's summer season. I was provided with an elephant, a koala, and a condor, and I brought Letty and my camel from home. The animals had to become comfortable with the stage on which we would be working, and with each other. In the weeks that followed Letty grew accustomed to new people, new surroundings, a sound system, an audience, and the many animals she would be working with during the next few months. It was pleasing to see how well she adapted, and the many guest trainers who appeared on the show were amazed at her temperament and behavior. Unknowing visitors would pass by and give her a pat on the hip. I would think to myself how surprised they would be if they should attempt that with another zebra.

Letty had such a busy month, I decided to incorporate that tendency into a trained behavior. A handkerchief was held up to her and when, out of curiosity, she touched it, I

Here, the difference in stripe pattern of the Hartmann's zebra, held by Joan, can be appreciated when compared to the Grévy's zebra, held by Duane.

Joan's relationship with Letty the zebra allows her to enjoy an association that few people have known.

gave her some grain. Next, I waited until she nibbled at it before rewarding her. From that point on, she had to pick it up before being rewarded. This is called training by approximation. Eventually, she would walk up and take the handkerchief out of a person's pocket, or fetch it off the ground, and bring it to me. In the show I would talk about the zebra's defenses of kicking and biting, at which time she would walk over to my co-host, Jerry, and grab a handkerchief from his hip pocket. Jerry was a professional announcer, not accustomed to wild animals, and a little nervous that Letty might decide to grab more than the handkerchief. When she finished the routine she would glance at me, waiting for her reward with her mouth open. Also, when I cleaned her run, if I set the rake down, she would pick it up and bring it to me.

When summer was over Letty returned to the ranch, and it was nice to be able to once again look out the window and see a zebra in the backyard. Fascination with their stunning beauty is something I will probably never lose.

Though all zebras look alike to most people, there are three primary types: plains zebras, mountain zebras, and Grévy's zebras. Each has a different striping pattern and comes from a different range, though in some areas ranges overlap. The most widespread and numerous are the plains (or common) zebras, so called because of the type of terrain in which they are found in East and Central Africa. Although their numbers have dropped in recent years, an estimated 300,000 roam the plains and savannahs from Southern Sudan to Northern South Africa. These zebras have shorter heads, smaller ears, and are more ponylike (13.2 hands) than their relatives.

Mountain zebras inhabit the mountain ranges of Southern Africa. They are small donkeylike animals that stand no more than twelve hands at the withers. Mountain zebras, like plains zebras, have broad stripes, but their bellies are white. They have a flap of skin, called a dewlap, on the underside of their necks, and horizontal bars in the pattern of a gridiron (football field) on their croup. There are two types of mountain zebras: the Hartmann's and the Cape. The Hartmann's are larger and their stripes are more widely spaced. Like the plains zebra, mountain zebras live in small herds. Often, groups mingle, graze together for a time, then move off, each band in its own direction. They are nonterritorial, nomadic, and migrate often. A herd stallion stands guard over five to fifteen mares and foals. Young stallions and those without herds of their own form bachelor herds. A dominance hierarchy exists within the family group. The herd provides safety to individuals from predators such as hyenas, lions, and hunting dogs. Yet, man is the greatest threat. During the last twenty years Hartmann's mountain zebras have dropped alarmingly from more than fifty thousand to fewer than five thousand, mainly due to competition with domestic livestock for food and water.

Grévy's zebras, also highly endangered, are the largest and most stunning of the three types of zebra. They have narrow stripes, large, rounded ears, and a broad dark dorsal stripe bordered by white. Found in the dry, hot, desert-fringe areas of Northern Kenya, Southern Ethiopia, and in three isolated parts of Somalia, they number only a few thousand. Although hunting and poaching have affected all zebras, the Grévy's, with its vivid narrow stripes, has been particularly valued for its skin, which has been made into wall hangings, rugs, purses, phone-book covers, coasters, and wallets. Since a poached skin can be sold for four hundred dollars to two thousand dollars, and because this activity is so difficult to control, the only way of saving the zebras seems to be to educate the potential buyers that the possession of a zebra-skin wallet does not justify the killing of one of these magnificent animals. Letty and Zelda are used during my television and public appearances to try and convince the public that zebras are much more pleasing to see in the flesh than on the floor of a game room.

Other creatures may also suffer from the zebra's demise. Because zebras prefer tough, coarse grass, as they eat, they expose the succulent green undergrass, which can then be consumed by gazelles, wildebeests, and other grazing animals.

Grévy's zebras, having the longest splint bones of any member of the horse family, are thought to possibly be the most primitive living equine. It also has been speculated that the earliest equids were spotted and striped and did not have solid coloration. The Grévy's narrow stripes are regarded as the most primitive coat pattern among living equines, while the zebras that evolved later had fewer and broader stripes. Grévy's zebras do not form permanent bonds, as do other species of zebra. Herds constantly change and solitary stallions are often territorial. This may represent the original form of social organization among equids, for Eohippus is presumed to have been territorial. Social bonds and group behavior followed later.

Each zebra's stripe pattern is as unique as are individual fingerprints in humans. It's hard to imagine that this vivid stripe pattern also serves as a type of camouflage. At a distance the stripes help to break the zebra's outline, blending it with the background. Stripes can be deceptive in herd situations, when zebras are tightly bunched. In the blur of movement, individuals are almost impossible to distinguish.

Zebras are resistant to common African diseases that affect horses. Therefore, efforts were made by government and private agencies to train them and cross them with horses and donkeys. However, because they were as resistant to training as they were to disease, these programs did not prove successful. While in the wild, zebra species do not interbreed; in captivity they have been crossed. Since each species has its own set of chromosomes—Grévy's zebra, 46; plains zebra, 44; mountain zebra, 32; domestic horse, 64; Przewalski's horse, 66—in almost all cases zebra hybrids are infertile. Of the horse- or pony-zebra crosses I have seen, the animal resembles the horse more, but with faint striping. They appear and behave somewhat mulelike. In my estimation, you end up with a bit of a freak, without the best of either side. They lack the beautiful color and characteristics of the zebra and are temperamentally less desirable than a horse.

Though there are a few trained zebras, I am sure there have been many more attempts than successes. I have heard stories by horse trainers of some wild zebra rides, most of which ended abruptly, never to be tried again. Exceptions to the rule are usually found in the circus.

At Circus World, in Florida, there are two zebras trained to pull a chariot. I spoke with their trainer, who explained that he had always worked them together as a pair. Singly they were difficult to control. Most trained zebras have been the common zebra, since the other species are endangered and to obtain and keep them requires special permits. I do have pictures of Mary Chipperfield working her impressive Liberty routine with three Grévy's zebras in her circus in England.

Most people are not able to obtain very young zebras, which means that by the time they do get one, it already has its wild personality. We had an advantage with Letty and Zelda because we were able to bottle-feed them and they came to think of us as their "mother." They became dependent on us for food and care and, although they are now much more independent, they still remember the past. It is much more difficult with an older animal.

You can muscle around a domestic horse and impress upon it that you're the boss. The zebra, however, fights discipline, and like most wild animals, eventually, with exhaustion, goes into a state of shock if pushed too far. In the

Joan and Letty at dusk, in the hills behind the ranch

wild, when zebras are caught by lions and hyenas, they seem to fight back at first, but then if they realize that they can't win, they appear to go into a trancelike state, at which time they may not even feel pain. In training zebras it is essential not to stress them to the point of shock, which could kill them. They must be gradually conditioned to restraint. One ranch tried to break an adult zebra to ride, and it ran into a fence and fractured its neck. Because of fear it was not able to handle intensive restraint psychologically. Riding and driving are forms of restraint totally contrary to the instincts of most wild animals. To them, restraint is a life-threatening situation. When restrained, they cannot defend themselves or flee.

Gradually, the flight distance of wild animals can be reduced with constant controlled exposure. Animals show stress in many ways—including posture, expression, breathing rate, and ear position. Sometimes the animal will give you a sign, but occasionally they react so quickly, there isn't time to respond. When people see a zebra walking down the street in a parade they usually say, ''Look, a tame zebra!'' It is true that a particular zebra may be more tame than a zoo animal or one in the wild. However, Zelda and Letty are far from being tame in the same way that a domestic equine is. The wild animal in them is just hiding beneath the surface, and the slightest outside stimulus could cause either of our mares to behave as though they were on the African veldt, not on a paved street in San Diego.

# MUSTANGS

As a romantic young girl I used to idealize the life of wild horses roaming free, owned by no one, tough and proud. Later, however, I was disillusioned when I learned the truth about their tenuous existence.

The mustang, the wild horse of the Americas, is in fact not truly wild, but feral, being a descendant of domestic animals introduced to this country by Spanish explorers in the early 1500s, and bred at mission ranches from which some of them escaped. Bands formed, the natural selection process took over, and they survived in and were molded by their harsh environment. The Plains Indians captured and redomesticated many of them, but the vast majority roamed wild and free across the prairies. Once numbering more than a million, by 1969 the mustang population dropped to fewer than seventeen thousand. From the 1930s until 1971, when the Wild Horse and Burro Act was passed, wild horses were under tremendous pressure from mustangers.

Mustangs have never been popular with ranchers, who have accused them of depleting the range, competing with livestock and big game, and luring away domestic mares. The fencing of ranges restricted the movement of wild horses, gradually forcing them west. Mustangs were shot, poisoned, caught, and broken. Professional mustangers captured them for pet food, and for export for human consumption in parts of Europe. Some were sold to rodeos at fifty to sixty cents per pound. An average horse brought $470 each (seven hundred to one thousand pounds). Their numbers declined and they became warier and tougher. They reached an all-time low in 1971.

Then, the climate of opinion changed. Humane groups began to call for their preservation. The Wild Horse and Burro Act put mustangers out of business, and wild horses were on the rise again. Regulated by the Bureau of Land Management, an agency of the Department of the Interior that oversees some 170 million acres of grazing land in the West, their numbers are monitored. It is through this agency that culling has taken place in recent years. The controversy continues over how the herds are to be managed. The Bureau of Land Management is caught between the conflicting interests of those who want mustangs left alone and those who want them controlled or removed altogether. The livestock and hunting industries resent mustangs, complaining that they eat public grass that could be used to feed domestic cattle, horses, and big game. Most ranchers' and hunters' philosophy can be simply stated: "If you can't hunt it, and you can't eat it, and you can't wear it—and I can't sell it—it should not be allowed on my public lands."

Supporters of mustangs believe that the animal is beautiful in itself and lends both aesthetic and historical value to the American landscape. They dispute the claim that mustangs are proliferating at an alarming rate. One research group has been testing antifertility drugs as a possible way to control mustang populations.

Meanwhile, roundups continue in the areas of greatest population density. The mustangs are herded into funnel-like trap fences, where they are then contained for health tests before being loaded into trucks and taken to adoption centers. The Adopt-A-Horse program began in 1973 as a humane method for disposing of excess horses. Since the program spread nationwide in 1976, more than forty thousand animals have been placed in foster homes across

Mustangs are the descendants of horses brought to America by Spanish explorers.

America. The fee for adoption of a wild horse is $125 plus transportation costs. A list of adoption centers may be obtained by writing the Bureau of Land Management, Denver Service Center, P.O. Box 25047, Denver, Colorado 80225. Adoption applicants must be legal residents of legal age, have no prior convictions for inhumane treatment of animals, and have adequate facilities and means of transportation.

Although this may seem like an inexpensive way to acquire a horse, it is important to remember that some mustangs suffer from malnutrition and all are wild animals, not accustomed to people. They remain the legal property of the Bureau of Land Management for one year, at which time the adoptee may apply for a title with a veterinarian's cer-

tification of proper care. Until this title is obtained the horse may not be sold. These animals often require a great deal of tender loving care to overcome their natural fears, especially of man. They fare best in the hands of experienced handlers. It is questionable if there will be enough qualified homes to place the number of horses yet to be culled. This process is very costly and there are no easy solutions for the future of the wild horse.

The status of the mustang is no different than the status of wildlife in many areas. Competition with humans for land space means we must re-evaluate our usage of land and resources and determine ways to co-exist.

31

# BREEDING

Horse breeding can be wonderfully rewarding, but the occasional disappointments are heartbreaking. Breeding is a creative process in which a stallion is chosen carefully for a particular mare with the hope that the product of that union will prove to be something special. On our ranch Duane and I breed miniature horses, Clydesdales, and Quarter Horses.

The birth of our first miniature foal was one of the most exciting moments in all my experiences with horses. We had moved our mare, Lakeside Lady, to a temporary foaling stall we had built on the porch outside our bedroom. I was able to see her from my bed, and I found myself waking with the slightest noise from her as I anticipated the coming birth. She settled in comfortably to her new surroundings and would even open the sliding screen door and enter the bedroom when she wanted attention. About two weeks passed, and as I was routinely walking down the hall one evening around nine o'clock, I heard her water break. I called for Duane and we both watched as the mare lay down and began to strain rhythmically. A small white bubble of membrane appeared through which the foal's front feet were visible, a welcome sign of a normal presentation. Within seconds the head emerged, and we were thrilled to see for the first time the foal we had awaited for eleven months. Within minutes the foal's entire body was visible and we could see we had a black colt. He was incredibly small compared to a standard-size foal. He weighed only sixteen pounds and stood eighteen inches tall, whereas a normal foal weighs about eighty pounds. As he struggled to his feet, still wet from the birth fluid, I wanted to put my arms around him. Lady nickered softly to him and began to clean him as he learned how to use his legs. I could hardly sleep that night I was so excited. I kept waking up to check on him and marvel at his tiny perfect body. What fun it was to watch him grow.

Later that year we again bred Lady, and following the same procedure, prepared for her foaling. This time she seemed more restless. One evening she lay down and began to strain, but rose again. I was a bit concerned and consulted our veterinarian about her unusual behavior. He suggested

Two new foals play in spring flowers.

For every new foal, an outing is an adventure.

*(Below)* Joan with Lad and his mare and daughter

*(Left)* Joan carries a sleepy two-day-old miniature foal to the barn.

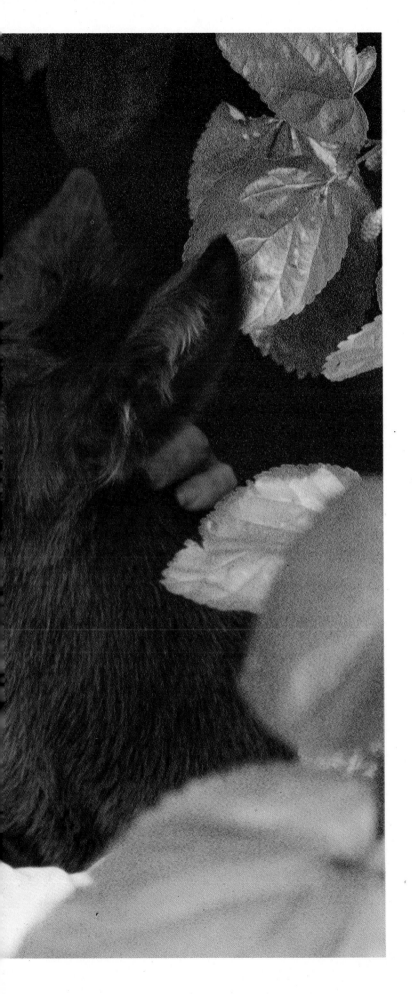

we keep a close watch on her. That evening she went down again, this time in heavy labor. As she pushed we looked for the front feet. To our alarm, as we approached to assist her we found only a tail, indicating a breech presentation. She was not able to deliver a foal in this position without help. Duane quickly called our veterinarian while I tried to find the feet by placing my arm inside her. I knew we were in trouble when I couldn't turn the foal. The veterinarian was on his way, and although he arrived within minutes, it seemed like forever. He quickly inserted his arm and, in time, was able to manipulate the foal so that he could deliver it by pulling. The veterinarian held its limp wet body as he checked for a heartbeat, but it had died. It was a terribly empty, helpless feeling of great loss. We were comforted by the fact that the mare seemed to be doing well and would be able to have more foals.

It is always guesswork when a mare will deliver. Sometimes it seems the mare will deliberately wait until no one is around. Most mares deliver in the late evening or early morning. The gestation period averages eleven months, but mares have been known to foal up to four weeks early or four weeks late. Impending birth signs include enlargement of the udder at two to six weeks before birth. As the udder firms, *waxing,* a waxy secretion from the nipples, may appear. The vulva will relax and elongate and the muscles on either side of the root of the tail will soften and sink slightly. These symptoms vary with each individual mare. One may show all symptoms, while in another they may be less pronounced or nonexistent.

When my Quarter Horse, Blitzann, came due this year, I watched for signs that she was close to foaling. Her milk bag filled, her hip muscles relaxed, and she was so heavy she acted as if it were uncomfortable to walk. She seemed ready to me, so I set up a watch schedule for every two hours. I would stay up until midnight, wake at two A.M., four A.M., and six A.M. She was too big to put on the porch like my miniature mare, so I had to walk out to the barn in freezing evening temperatures to check her. It seemed as soon as I was warm and comfortable, it was time to get up again. Her estimated foaling date passed, and after two weeks I was beginning to wear down. I wondered if she was ever going to foal. On the third week as I arrived home from work, I first went to the barn. There lay Blitzann having just delivered her foal, who was still encased in the birth sac. It was sputtering for air, so I quickly entered and opened the sac, lifting the foal's head and clearing its mouth. I stepped back and watched as it took its first breath and whinnied to the mare. As it rose I was pleased to see it was a beautiful bay filly. She was so large she looked as if she were weeks old—definitely a foal worth waiting for.

To Joan every new foal is special.

# BEHAVIOR

The horse is a creature of instinct, and his survival instincts were developed over the centuries by wild ancestors who had to contend with predatory animals and environmental hazards. Although most of the original stimuli have long been absent, their influence on the horse is evident in the behavior of domestic stallions, mares, and foals. An equine's brain is relatively small in relation to its size, and the horse acts more from instinct than from reason. When this premise is accepted, it becomes easier to understand the horse and to train him. Highly developed senses—particularly hearing, sight, and smell—and a built-in flight-oriented defense help to explain the excitable nature of the horse. Diet, exercise, handling, and individual temperament also have considerable influence on the behavior of a horse.

Horses have a deeply rooted herd instinct that offers security in the wild, partly by providing a collective warning system. Their inclination to follow is evident on the racetrack and the trail. A horse that might otherwise balk at crossing a stream or natural barrier will follow another horse over the same obstacle. When a horse gets loose, he will run to others. In the herd a dominant stallion exerts discipline over his band, and submission allows for an acceptance of discipline. Fortunately, horses appear to accept the dominance of man in substitution for the herd leader, and when properly handled they will trust him as a creature upon whom their well-being depends. At times, however, even as they would have done in the herd, equines will test the authority of the leader. Resistances of horses in training are examples of this testing. When met with quiet firmness, the desire to dominate is usually overcome easily, but if animals are once allowed to succeed with resistance, they will take advantage of the situation, thereafter attempting to reverse the roles of leader and follower. In training horses it is important to remember that mental development is just as important as physical development.

The most easily read signals of the mood of a horse are flagged by the ears, which usually provide an accurate indication of what to expect. Ears pointed forward sharply indicate tension, curiosity, and good intentions. Laterally

Joan's experience with Letty gives her a deeper insight into her domestic horses.

flapped-out ears show boredom or fatigue, if relaxed, and anger if they are tense. Ears that are pressed flat against the mane are a warning of massive aggression. Between these extreme positions lies a whole range of subtle signals, all probably easily understood by equines, but difficult for man to read. Combinations of positions are often used in moments of anxiety or uncertainty. The ears also provide a subtle means of communication between equines—one animal receiving a message about the location of a sound stimulus by glancing at the position of another horse's ears.

Aside from ear positions, facial expressions so subtle they are hardly distinguishable by humans are probably the most important visual signals used in communication between animals. Nose flaring, muzzle wrinkling, and jaw flexing play an important part in the communication of horses. The sticking out or tightening of the lips, the angle of curve at the edge of the mouth, and the number of teeth shown are everyday means of mute communication among animals. The ability to perceive even the slightest movement allows horses to read signals generally indiscernible to the human eye.

Body signals, a more obvious means of communication, are easier for a human to decipher. An outstretched neck accompanied by ears laid back and head swung to the side is a common threat gesture. A horse usually threatens to kick by hunching the back slightly and pushing up or working a hind leg. Stallions arch their necks to impress other horses. Mares adopt the sawhorse position to express sexual receptiveness, and they also lift their tails for the same reason. A threatened subordinate horse will often tuck its tail between its legs, while a displaying stallion lifts his. Swishing a tail back and forth aggressively can mean discomfort or threat and warning. An entire herd of horses will usually become alarmed if they see one horse in an alerted position—weight brought evenly onto all four feet, tail partly raised, and ears pointed forward. Shaking the head vigorously up and down is frequently an indication of inhibited aggression by a horse that is undecided whether to approach or to flee from an unidentified intruder.

In the wild, body language is probably the most used form of equine communication, whereas on a ranch or in a stable, a horse has to rely almost entirely on his voice. This is because he is contained and does not have visual access to the other horses. Vocalization is usually heard with the introduction of a new horse to the stable. Stallions will vocalize to mares coming into season. Mares and foals will call to each other, especially if separated. Because of their association with humans, they will even nicker if they recognize a person, or if they need something. For example, at feeding time when I walk into the barn, many of the horses will vocalize to let me know they want their meal. If I open a grain bin in the feedroom, I'm almost sure to hear a response from the barn.

The most often used horse vocalization is the whinny, or neigh. I generally think of it as a greeting. Often, horses that are new arrivals to a ranch or stable will whinny continuously, which may be caused by nervousness or the stress of a new situation and surroundings. A whinny is also used as a distance call. When someone rides past our ranch, our horses whinny to the strange animal. The nicker differs from the loud whinny by being a soft call or greeting. It's often heard when a mare talks to her foal. Sometimes, horses in the barn will nicker in a sort of greeting—as a response to my presence. It is a more subtle type of greeting or communication. The squeal is heard primarily from stallions, although sometimes mares squeal as a signal of rejection to a stallion. They may squeal and kick if they don't want a stallion to approach. Horses that are arguing or fighting with one another also squeal. A snort is frequently heard when a horse is alarmed or frightened. It is an alert response. When a horse is let out to run, it sometimes seems to snort with excitement. A horse expresses the sigh by taking a deep breath and expelling air between its vibrating lips. It usually signifies contentment. Frequently, if a horse is worked in a tense situation then rewarded with a pat, it will respond with the sigh to show that it has relaxed. Another noise made with air exhalations is the blow, which is often used by displaying stallions.

There is some controversy as to whether a horse really vocalizes in recognition of his owner. This, I think, is an individual response depending on the sort of relationship a horse has with his master. For example, there's a big difference between Finally, the horse that I raised from a weanling and worked with every single day of his life, and most of the other horses in our barn who have had different owners. When I arrive home, Finally is the only horse that puts his head out of the stall and whinnies to me. To acknowledge his greeting I frequently give him attention, and occasionally offer him grain or one of his favorite foods. Many people tend to read their own thoughts into the mind of their horse, imagining behavior and responses that don't exist. It is easy to give human characteristics to animals, imagining them to be what we wish them to be and not what they are.

Obviously, close rapport can be achieved between horses and people, and there are those special animals that relate closely to people and respond accordingly. In this respect, Finally, for example, cannot be compared to my Thoroughbred, Eagle, who appears to associate people with a means to an end: to get out and be exercised, and to be fed and watered. His attitude seems to be, "Let's do the work and leave me alone." He doesn't like to be groomed and he doesn't care for attention. He simply doesn't seem to need closeness or affection from people. Between him and Finally there is a wide range of man-horse associations. Most horses are somewhere in between, some are extremely affectionate, and others are not. Some may be excellent performing horses; Eagle is a good jumper and a very athletic

All equines self-groom, removing oil, dead hair, and skin from their hides by rolling in dust.

horse. However, he will work for me only because he is willing and not because he is seeking to please a human being.

When horses are trained in a captive situation, they don't have the chance to flee. Their flight distance becomes almost nonexistent. Often, they are placed into situations completely contrary to their natural instincts: being tied up, being contained in a stall, being saddled, and having a rider. When a horse reaches its maximum tolerance level, it is not unusual for it to short-circuit and, in spite of all training, resort to its flight reaction, which seems to vary temperamentally from one animal to another. Although we are able to impose our will on a once wild equine, and although the animal seems accepting of the demands that we put on him, if pushed beyond a certain point his natural instinct will override his training.

The best wild animals in shows are exceptional to their species; they are definitely not the norm. They are usually extremely mellow, accepting animals and may very well be the creatures who would not have survived in the wild because they have a delayed reaction flight time. For the purposes of a show, however, they may excel in accepting training demands, and they may also have the stamina, the desire, and the ability to take the initiative. A good example of this is the cutting horse, who has to be accepting of a handler or a trainer and, yet, when his cow sense comes into play, he must be able to respond independently of his rider.

Deviant behaviors in captive horses are usually the result of boredom or mishandling. Man must accept full responsibility for stall kickers, cribbers, weavers, and windsuckers.

A horse in the wild spends most of its time seeking food, traveling for water, and interacting with members of the herd. Horses that are tough to ride and have bad habits, such as bucking, can often be helped by giving them lots of exercise. My horse Eagle, for instance, may attempt to toss me off if he is not worked frequently. He will buck almost maliciously when he is feeling good. Yet, when he is worked on a regular basis, he can be a pleasure to ride.

Some people seem to get along well with a certain type of horse. A horse that is calm needs someone to push him on, and a less composed horse will respond to a rider who is quiet and reassuring. Good teamwork is when horse and rider are well matched, with temperaments that complement one another.

Leo is a well-mannered stallion who rarely causes problems. I remember one afternoon when we took him and one of our geldings out for a ride. Leo behaved himself, but the situation changed on the next day's ride, when a mare joined Leo and the gelding. At one point the mare was separated from Leo when the gelding got between them, and Leo responded with natural stallion behavior by dropping his head, pinning his ears, and charging the gelding. Because we had never seen him be aggressive, at first we weren't aware why he had gone after the gelding. A few minutes later, however, when the gelding again separated him from the mare, we realized it was her presence that had caused Leo to behave in a possessive and aggressive manner. It was a good example of how important it is to understand the horse's natural behavior if we are to deal with him in a domestic situation.

# HORSE SHOWS

The animal shows at the San Diego Zoo and Wild Animal Park were planned to present a philosophy of conservation and to develop an appreciation for wildlife. Visitors could always view elephants in an enclosure, but to see them actually move logs, to learn something of their history and capabilities, and to see them use their intelligence, gave people more insight into the true nature of the animals. The shows also provided entertainment that would draw people into the park. My first experience with animal shows was primarily with elephants. Later, I worked with mixed groups of wild animals. As the Wild Animal Park developed, it was decided to add a horse show to the existing bird and elephant shows.

Though a horse show might seem out of place in a park featuring exotic animals, the tremendous impact of humans on wild animal populations is no better illustrated than by a look at the domestic horse breeds that have been derived from wild stock. Not only has man influenced the development of the domestic horse, the horse has had a tremendous effect on the history of mankind.

When the original horse show trainer left the Wild Animal Park, I was offered the job. I was being asked to do something I have always wanted to do—and be paid for it. Since horses were so important to me, I jumped at this chance, which proved very challenging. It gave me the opportunity to pursue my varied interests with all different breeds of horses. I wanted to demonstrate the diversity of horses, their interaction with man, and their evolutionary process. Time was short, for I only had a couple of months to put the entire show together, hire and find representative breeds of horses that could not only work under the conditions of the park, but also fit our budget. To get the ball rolling, I decided to use some of my own horses; at least I knew what they could do. It was difficult to narrow down our choice of breeds, but we tried to obtain a good representation by taking into account size, color, gait, and style of work.

First, we accustomed the horses to the area in which the show was to be presented. It sounds easy, but at the Wild Animal Park we never knew when an elephant would come

Diamond does a camel stretch bow cued by a tap on the withers.

Lad, a miniature stallion, can walk almost fifty feet on his hind legs.

walking around the corner, and there was always the loose waterbuck, along with peacocks and various types of waterfowl. Even worse, we had to contend with the traffic, because just behind our exhibition area was the major service center for the park.

Once the horses were settled in, we began training sessions with small audiences until we were ready to open for the public. We choreographed the training with a script that I had written using appropriate music for each segment. We tried to give our audiences a feel for each breed and aspect of horsemanship without lingering too long, since the park's philosophy was that most people, without becoming restless or bored, can't sit through a program that lasts longer than twenty minutes. It was a real challenge to show fifty million

years of equine evolution and man's relationship with the horse in less than a half hour. We managed to exhibit ten different breeds and eight different styles of horse work, utilizing the proper tack for each animal and with the riders dressed in appropriate attire. With a limited budget it was quite a challenge not only to obtain the correct gear but also to find suitable animals.

Shows were presented three to four times a day, seven days a week. The greatest problem with doing daily shows was the consistency factor. To find a horse that will be consistent day after day is extremely difficult. Animals, like people, have good days and bad days. What we attempted to accomplish through our training were horses that would give maximum performances for each show.

We found it was extremely important to keep the animals guessing just enough to keep a little spontaneity in each performance. A horse too familiar with a routine may become ring sour. If that happens, the entire act may have to be rechoreographed, which could involve changing music, the script, and possibly the whole show. A good example of how horses become too familiar with routine may be illustrated by a dressage exhibition we had in our show. The horse knew that he would be asked to do a half-pass, a dressage movement, at a certain point in the ring, for every show. Day after day he did this routine until he began to anticipate the half-pass before he arrived at the designated spot, and before we gave him his cue. The problem then became complicated because we ended up cueing the horse *not* to do the behavior that he had been trained to do and which he knew was expected of him. In a show such as ours, problems like this were magnified by the fact that unless we wanted to work seven days a week, someone else had to ride that same horse on each of our free days. Everyone had a slightly different style, even though we were doing the same routines, and it was impossible for each rider to cue in exactly the same manner. Also, each horse performed a little better or worse for one person than for another. The horses had to adjust to different styles of riding and different riders day to day and show to show.

The Wild Animal Park show started with the Przewalski's horse, also known as the Mongolian wild horse. We used our Przewalski mare to demonstrate the true wild horse as it existed before its involvement with man. We pointed out the similarities between her and zebras and wild asses, and compared each to the modern horse.

Next, we talked about how the horse gave man the mobility to conquer lands and establish new civilizations. To the theme song of *How the West Was Won*, our Quarter Horse, with a pack mule in tow, made his way down a steep hillside into the arena. We then reviewed the development of the Quarter Horse breed from use in ranch work to racing.

Finally was the first horse Joan ever taught to rear.

It is important that a horse's rear is controlled so the handler can be in close proximity without being hurt.

Quarter Horses were once famous for being the breed that could run a quarter mile fastest. After descending the hillside, the mule was tethered, and the horse was maneuvered to a gate which the mounted rider opened, then closed before working through a series of obstacles placed on the ground. The horse was asked to back up and sidepass through parallel poles, and then to walk through tires by carefully placing his feet through the center of each of them, which showed trust and control between horse and rider. The horse was next put through each of the Western gaits— walk, jog, and lope—in order to compare his styles to the gaits of other breeds used later in the show.

As a horse and rider entered the arena, the rider's dress, as well as the tack on the horse, were explained in order to show their relevance to the type of work being done. For example, chaps are worn to protect a cowboy's legs, and the horn on the Western saddle is for dallying (tying) a rope. Other dress might include a hat, gloves, scarf, boots, jacket, and pants for the rider; and bits, saddles, hobbles, and even braiding in the mane and tail for the horse.

The next horse shown was Eagle, a Thoroughbred, the breed that has the largest registry in the United States. They are not only the fastest distance running horses in the world, but also excel in jumping. We demonstrated how to train a horse to jump with cavallettis, or ground poles, which are used to teach stride and confidence crossing over an obstacle. The cavallettis are raised gradually, and eventually a fence is introduced. Poles may be added in order to increase height or width of an obstacle. In the show, when we cleared a four-foot jump with a four-foot spread, people were really able to see the athletic ability of a Thoroughbred. We explained the difference between hunters, jumpers, and combined training horses, and showed English gaits and the appropriate riding attire.

In the performance, to demonstrate a breed that has been selected for color, we used a leopard Appaloosa. The Nez Percé Indians developed the Appaloosa for its flashy spotted coat. A leopard Appaloosa has spots covering its entire body, as opposed to some Appaloosas that have just a few spots, or possibly a blanket of spots on the hindquarters. We also used the Appaloosa to demonstrate a style of horse competition known as gymkhana. In this case, he and his rider performed a pole-bending routine, weaving in and out of a line of six upright poles approximately twenty feet apart. A timed event, it was thrilling to watch. These competitive games on horseback that are used today for recreation were once practiced by the Indians to train for battle.

Next, we brought out the giant of the horse world. Our Clydesdale mare named Melody was chosen to represent the draft-horse breeds. Draft horses were selected for size, and originally developed to carry knights in armor, who weighed up to four hundred pounds. Later, they were used as work horses on farms and in industry. Melody stood eighteen hands (a hand being equal to four inches) at the shoulder and weighed about eighteen hundred pounds. She pulled a heavy drag, hooked to her harness, to smooth the surface of the arena. To emphasize her stature, a miniature horse, which stood twenty-eight inches high and weighed about ninety pounds, was brought into the ring. Seeing these two animals standing together, it was easy to appreciate the effect of selective breeding.

Not only have horses been bred for speed, color, and size, but also for a particular gait. To show this feature we introduced a Tennessee Walking Horse, selectively bred for a special four-beat "running walk," which is very comfortable to ride even at speed. These horses, which were originally ridden by Southern plantation owners when they inspected their crops, can walk as fast as some horses trot, and can continue for long periods of time without tiring.

The oldest breed, the Arabian, was shown under sidesaddle. What a pretty picture it was to see such a refined horse carrying a beautiful woman dressed in a long, flowing skirt, a matching coat with lace cuffs and choker, and a top hat. It was a reminder of days past and of how, along with the times, styles have changed, influencing our perception of the horse.

Another type of riding that was demonstrated was dressage. This routine was performed to classical music and the rider wore formal attire. We also showed driving, with a Shetland Pony hitched to a pony cart.

The finale to our performance was a circus Liberty routine, in which a half Arabian (Finally) entered the ring wearing a black patent leather harness and black and red ostrich feathers on its headpiece. He waltzed, marched, did changes of direction, then stood on his hind legs and took a bow, all of which was done with only the slightest direction from his handler, who was standing in the center of the ring. As he finished his routine, the entire cast of the show came out to give the audience a close look at the tremendous variety of animals that comprise the horse world.

Actually, performing in the ring was a small part of the work involved in putting on our exhibition. Because each animal was turned out as it would be in a formal horse show, we spent the first three hours of every morning washing and grooming the animals. We also had to scrub and oil all the tack, and polish the silver. Then the arena had to be dragged, and the cavallettis and jumps set. At thirty minutes per show, it seemed that most of our time was spent cleaning. The toughest days were those when it was 110 degrees hot, or freezing cold, because we had no cover for shade or to protect us from rain.

The Wild Animal Park horse show helped the public to see that there is something of value in each of the different equine traits. Quarter Horse people turn up their noses at gaited horses, Arabian enthusiasts have little interest in draft horses, mini-horse people have their idea of what a horse should look like. We were trying to go beyond all those subjective opinions and demonstrate that the horse isn't one thing, the horse is sixty breeds. We did not have the budget, the time, or the expertise to show the very best; it would have been impossible. However, we were able to help people understand why no other animal has been more important to mankind.

During our shows, things frequently went wrong. Since I couldn't afford the luxury of a champion sidesaddle rider who couldn't ride Western, jumping, or work a Liberty horse, each rider had to be able to ride every style. There were times when we had to pinch-hit; there were riders who were better in different areas. The Western riders helped the English riders and the English riders helped the Western riders; each of us had to be able to know and manage every single animal.

At a show one day, I was riding my Thoroughbred when he started bucking, rearing, and acting up until I was forced to discipline him, at which time he threw me off. There was dead silence—you could have heard a pin drop. I got right back on and continued riding. There was quite a crowd of people watching, but I just couldn't take him back and tie him up and wait until later to punish him. I had to let him know right then that I meant business and he couldn't get away with misbehaving. If I had ignored his disobedience it would have only reinforced his poor behavior. It's been said, and I tend to agree, that you are either training or untraining every time you work a horse, or any other ani-

(Above) Here, Joan leads Letty onstage for a show at the San Diego Zoo.

(Left) It is her ability to express her knowledge of and love for animals that has given Joan such a large following.

mal. You're either reinforcing a behavior that you want or you are showing them that they can do what they want.

I am sure that when the horses went into the arena they knew exactly what was expected of them. They knew when it was five minutes before a show, they knew each rider's capabilities, they knew that the public was there. In fact, they were so well trained, they were ready to go in themselves and do the routine on their own. At the end of the day they knew it was time to return to their stalls. Sometimes we'd just free them and they'd go to the barn by themselves!

After giving so much of ourselves to the horse show in daily performances for three years, it was not easy to live with the decision of the zoo to replace the horse show with another series of animal acts. It was one of the most difficult times in my career at the zoo. I remember I went down to the credit union, took out the biggest loan I could get, and bought as much tack and as many horses as I possibly could. I just couldn't bear to see them go. We tried to find the best possible homes for the horses—though I would have liked to have taken them all.

# TELEVISION

Television enables me to share my experiences with animals with millions of people. Working in this medium can be at the same time both exciting and frightening. Through guest spots on TV talk shows, I have been able to show hundreds of different animal species, including equines. Unlike many animals trained for specific uses in commercials and movies, my animals are often untrained and may never have appeared on TV before, nor will they ever appear again.

Every time I take an animal on a television show it is a unique experience. I never know exactly how it is going to respond until we are in the studio. There is nothing worse than having a problem in front of television cameras transmitting the entire scene to twenty million people. Before going on a show I try to imagine all the possible complications and how to avoid them, as well as what I would do should a problem occur. Most shows today are taped live and aired later. Whatever happens, happens, and that is what is aired. With production costs on major shows running up to many thousands of dollars, they can't afford to stop tape to work out problems. This creates a great deal of pressure because once the cameras are rolling, it's too late to make changes. If mistakes are made and a performer is not reliable, he doesn't get asked back to do more shows. I have tried to develop credibility by being on time and in control, with healthy, well-groomed animals that behave more or less as they have been represented.

Formats vary from show to show, but generally, a guest segment runs five to fifteen minutes. The time passes quickly, so it is important to get to the point and show the animal to its best advantage in as short a time as possible. The goal of most shows is to entertain, not to educate. My goal is to share with people some of the fascinations of the animal world, and I have to evaluate each particular animal and decide which of its characteristics are the most interesting, relevant, and important. When there is time I am able

Merv Griffin welcomes Joan and an emu on his show.

Johnny Carson gave Joan her start in television. She has appeared on his show more than forty times.

to go into more detail. It would be easy to appear on camera for five minutes and never say anything pertinent about the animal. On the other hand, a curious host may ask whatever comes to mind, so it is important to be prepared for any questions. Regardless of whether a host is comfortable with animals, I am responsible for his well-being, as well as that of the animals. For example, whether a particular animal has a tendency to bite or kick is something that obviously must be explained to the host before the show.

Zelda, our Grévy's zebra, is very handy with her hind legs and reluctant to trust strangers, so whenever I use her on a show, I have to make sure that the host gives a wide berth to her hindquarters and comes up to her head to pet her. Her head must always be positioned toward the host. Frequently, we use food so that Zelda will focus her attention on it and not be worried about what goes on around her.

Appearing on some shows with certain animals is like sitting on a time bomb. I know the danger capability of the animal and its attention span; I know that I have only a short time to show and explain everything, and I have to watch the animal, the audience, and all of the studio equipment while trying to answer questions. As I go onto the set I walk from semidarkness into the bright stage lights, which may partially blind the animal. Sometimes this works in my favor, because at that particular moment the animal may not really know where it is. Very quickly, though, it begins to assess the situation. Suddenly, it has been walked into a

new environment, from backstage to in front of an audience and three cameras that are moving, trying to obtain both close-ups and wide shots. The band may be sitting quietly or moving around, ruffling the pages of their music in order to prepare for their next song. The sound boom may suddenly be lowered from overhead. Animals see all of this. They see somebody flashing the cue cards to let the performers know how many minutes remain before the cameras begin to roll. The director and all the assistants are milling about. What you see on your television set is only a small section of the overall studio, which is full of distractions and movement. There are many variables that can affect an animal's attention and how well it behaves.

I felt fortunate just to be able to work with a Przewalski horse at the zoo, but to be able to take Bosaga to a television show and share her with millions of people was an even more special experience. The preparations for taking Bosaga on the *Tonight* show started early in the morning with bathing, grooming, and loading her into a trailer in San Diego. Next, we had to drive 125 miles of freeway to Los Angeles, with cars zooming by us at 55 miles an hour, bumper to bumper, where there was always the fear that someone would slam on his brakes in front of us. Twelve to fourteen hours passed from the time we left the zoo until we returned—this included the three hours it took to get to the show, the time it took at the studio to prepare for the show and to tape the show, and the time it took to get cleaned up and back to the zoo. Those twelve hours were full of tension.

Though most people think it would be great fun to work with animals on television, I never really relax until we are home, knowing that everything went well. Then I can begin to enjoy the experience. One of the most difficult things about such appearances is that many television people do not understand animals. In the case of Bosaga, for example, few people could realize how protective the management at the zoo was of this animal which, to the average eye, has the appearance of a donkey. It would be unfair to expect the production people to understand Bosaga's tremendous value and the importance of her being one of maybe only four hundred Przewalski horses in captivity. The minds of the studio crew were focused on getting the show on the air, and obtaining an hour or ninety minutes of tape. Naturally, the least of their concerns were my problems dealing with the animal. They were doing their job and expected me to do mine. Part of my job was to anticipate what they wanted, and to do my best to provide them with it, while at the same time being concerned mostly with their safety and that of the animal.

If I learn during practice that the band bothers the animal, then I have to ask the director to cut the music while the animal is on the air or have the musicians play very softly. Because animals attract a lot of attention backstage, they can create a problem. Naturally, everyone in the studio wants to see the zebras. A zebra or Przewalski gets tired after spending three hours on the road. If strange people are trying to pet it and fool around with it, by the time it goes on the air it may be cranky and difficult. The animal must be given a little space to rest and settle down.

I feel tremendously fortunate to be able to take animals on television, which can be, if used properly, the most effective of mass media educational devices. With Bosaga, for instance, I was able to introduce most people for the first time to a rare horse, and inform them why its survival depends on how well we are able to understand it and breed it in a captive situation. On an important national show, most of the thirty million viewers, if they are legal voters, may have a say in the future of our wildlife. Many people might ask, "It's an entertainment show. What are you doing there?" Well, my mission is to tell as many people as I can about animals, and if television provides the largest audience, that's where I go. Some hosts, like Merv Griffin, who have horses, have an interest in animals and not only allow me sufficient time, but will guide the conversation into areas about which I wish to speak. Others seem to have little idea of why I am on the show, and then it is my job to try to keep animals the center of conversation.

Although most of the national shows are taped in Los Angeles, I occasionally have to fly as far as New York with animals for a television appearance. Sometimes I have to travel alone and don't have people to help me get ready. Under these circumstances, my job is not as glamorous as it might appear. I have to get up in the dark, bathe animals, and clean cages. I might be in a motel room and have to haul all the animals and their crates downstairs and find transportation to the studio. Sometimes it is freezing cold, and the animals have to be kept happy and fed, cleaned, entertained, and not allowed to be destructive. When I'm traveling with animals, my entire attention and all of my time is spent on them. There simply isn't any time to go out and have fun in a new city.

When shows are taped on location at the zoo, the Wild Animal Park, my ranch, or in the field, it is much easier on the animals and I have greater flexibility, although there are some inherent problems, such as weather, extraneous sound, and variable light. I prefer shooting on location, although waiting for the right shot can be uncomfortable when working on a 110-degree day with reflectors, which intensify the heat. Even so, the results are usually worth the effort.

Taking a large animal on a television show presents the major challenge of getting it into the studio and, once inside, standing it safely on the stage. Footing is a problem with horses and other hoof stock, because most of the studio floors are very slick, and frequently highly polished. This requires me to carefully plan how to move the animal to the

Here, a black leopard demonstrates apprehension of Merv Griffin's approach by showing its teeth.

stage, which could be just inside the back door or a couple of hundred feet down a hallway.

I have two systems for moving an animal on a slippery surface. If the animal is small enough, I transport it on a large carpeted dolly with wheels, which can be rolled into the studio. If the animal cannot be moved on a dolly, I use twelve-foot by twelve-foot sections of indoor-outdoor carpeting. The animal is walked onto a section of carpet, then moved forward to a second section while the first section is moved in front of the second. The carpet sections are rotated one by one until the animal is backstage. Once there, it becomes a chore to keep the animal on the carpet until it appears on the air. We use runners on which to walk the animal from backstage to a carpeted area onstage. Sometimes it is difficult to restrain an animal on a relatively small section of rug. In three steps a horse can be off the safety of the pad and, if it moves rapidly and its hooves hit the slick floor, it may lose balance and possibly fall. There are rubber shoes made for horses, but it is difficult to find any that properly fit wild equines with odd-shaped feet.

When I appear with an animal that I know well and have worked closely on a daily basis, I am aware of what it does best, its expressions, its movements, its unique qualities. It

On *Sun-Up San Diego*, Joan introduces Letty to the show's hosts.

is not easy, however, to demonstrate these things in a short period of time, after a stressful journey and waiting for a long time backstage.

Suddenly, you're on the air and the animal is expected to turn on. On a live show in a studio, you can't sit and wait for the action that you want as though you were shooting on location. There, scenes can be repeated until you obtain what you want, or they can later be edited. When you're on live, what happens each moment is what is seen by the audience. If there is a problem, the most has to be made of the situation because the audience is watching. I try to relate to what is happening at the moment—if an animal becomes startled by the monitor because it sees movement there, I attempt to talk about perception and the alert position. Sometimes I might be trying to make an important point about conservation just when the animal will do something funny and the entire audience will laugh. Then, the host will naturally relate with humor to the incident at the very moment when I'm trying to be serious. On the other hand, if you are too serious and preachy and the audience interest drops, the host or director will signal for the next guest. Somehow, you have to keep things moving and entertaining while at the same time trying to make a constructive statement.

One of the most disappointing things that can happen in television is when so much work is put into preparation, a long trip is made, and then for some reason the show runs long, my segment is shortened, and an animal doesn't go on the air. There isn't anything more frustrating than putting work and time into preparing for a show and then not having it materialize. Animals themselves can be disappointing when a particular behavior or performance is anticipated but doesn't happen. Not long ago I suffered such an experience when Mike Douglas was shooting at the zoo. During lunch break we were discussing what animals we could introduce to him on camera, those that could be touched and handled. I went to great lengths to brag about Letty, the Hartmann's mountain zebra, telling how she was the best zebra I'd ever seen, and about all the shows on which she had appeared. I was certain I could lead her up to Mike, who would be able to pet her and to hold her leadrope.

When I went to get Letty she was feeling frisky, and I should have known then that I was in for trouble. Just as I led her up to Mike, she wheeled around and kicked at him, and if that weren't enough she wanted to chew his clothes, and simply wouldn't stand still. After having bragged so much about her, everything she could do wrong, she did wrong. She was just impossible to work. That was the first time she had ever acted that badly and she hasn't behaved as poorly since. She even reared up and struck at Mike with her front feet. No animal is completely predictable.

Every time an animal is taken on a live TV show, potential danger or embarrassment is just around the corner. Everything may seem to be going well when suddenly I notice that the zebra's hind foot is half off the carpet. There is a moment of panic when I realize that in just one step she could lose her balance, slip, and fall. Then, it is essential to remain calm, and inconspicuously move the zebra until her foot is back in position. This, however, may sound easier than it is, for if care is not taken, the zebra could just as easily step backward and off of the carpet, rather than forward and into safety. In this case, just twelve inches of carpet can be the difference between a successful show and a disaster. Although I think most people are fascinated with animals and watch my shows for that reason, still many people tune in just to see what is going to happen. There's that element of surprise: What is that animal going to do next? A wild animal on live TV provides the unexpected. If something goes wrong, what am I going to do? What is the host going to do? People know that we're not dealing with a contrived situation—this is live, this is what is happening now, and no one ever knows what is going to happen next.

Some of the instances when the animals I have presented behaved spontaneously have been moments that people seem to have remembered for years. I think the time that the marmoset jumped out of my hands and onto Johnny Carson's head, and then proceeded to mark that territory, went down in history as one of the funniest, most remembered pieces we've ever done on television. It's that fine line between great spontaneity and being out of control that people find fascinating. The marmoset, for example, could have just as easily jumped from Johnny Carson's head to the sound boom or the curtain, which could have resulted in a wild-goose chase. It was one of those instances when luck was in my favor and everyone seemed to feel that it was a fantastic show. From a personal standpoint, I am perfectly happy to have my presentations go quietly and not have anything spectacular happen, because I feel more comfortable with animals when things are under control. Those moments of exciting spontaneity may fascinate and amuse the television viewers, but they make my heart pound.

Since many people don't understand animal behavior and mistakenly think of me as a sort of Sheena, Queen of the Jungle, who can do everything with creatures, from zebras to lions, we often receive some unusual requests for appearances. Sometimes a director or producer will want something bizarre. Once I was asked to bring a live eighteen-foot giraffe to a television show. Another time someone wanted to use our zebra (who enjoyed kicking out at strangers) for an MTV commercial in which, as a rock group played, people would be dancing all around her in a disco.

One of the wonderful things about working for the zoo, as opposed to being an independent commercial animal handler whose living depends on how many jobs he is able to book for his animals, is that as a zoo employee, my first concern is for the well-being of the animal. I've never felt pressured into doing a risky show and taking more chances than I thought I could handle. The zoo allows me to use my own discretion and to do whatever I think will work best. That's nice. However, I can certainly empathize with commercial trainers who need money to pay those expensive food bills, and who may feel pressured to take on a job that requires risky situations bordering on the unreasonable.

# WORKING HORSES WITH OTHER ANIMALS

Working horses with other animals, such as camels, zebras, elephants, and even tigers in some circus acts, is best accomplished by gaining control over each animal before any attempts are made to introduce them. Resistance is natural at first and should be prepared for and expected. Attempts should be made to avoid pushing animals too fast because they tend to remember the bad experiences much longer than the good ones. Individual temperament is also a factor. A high-strung, nervous horse, for example, will be more difficult to handle in stressful situations than a calm animal. Working conditions should be arranged to ensure maximum control. Possible problems should be thought out beforehand and the trainer should be ready to act if they occur. Back-up help may also be essential to accomplish the training behavior. As progress is made, some of the controls may be dropped. What people don't see when they watch a finished animal act are the many step-by-step stages of training that were necessary to make the finished performance successful.

Some of the most impressive and unusual combinations of horses working with other animals occur in the circus. Gunther Gebel Williams, in the Ringling Bros. and Barnum & Bailey Circus, worked two horses with three tigers and an African elephant in one forty-foot ring. It took Gunther three years to assemble and train the animals in this mixed act, the only one of its kind. The tigers were hand raised, the elephant raised from a baby, and the horses very carefully chosen. In the act two tigers leap to the horses' backs, which are padded. The cats then ride around the ring before sitting up simultaneously when the horses stop. The third tiger rides on the elephant's back. The horses and the elephant both have a natural fear of predators, which must

On her ranch Joan has an unusual variety of animals. Here, Tuffy the dog and Rookie the macaw appear with Lad.

*(Pages 58 and 59)* Joan introduces Finally to Montgomery the bobcat, given to her by the Montgomery Zoo in Alabama.

be overcome. Gunther also works horses together with elephants.

In the Circus Vargas, Rex Williams directs three rings of elephants from horseback. It is amazing to watch him and his horse ride around and between the huge elephants, keeping each animal in its place. Few trainers have the ability to perfect such spectacular displays. There are many people who train elephants and many who train horses, but few like Gunther and Rex, who have the vision, ability, and courage to go beyond the normal parameters of training. One wrong move could be disastrous. Top trainers know their animals so well they can usually anticipate what they will do before they do it. Behind every great act is a great trainer.

My first experience working a horse directly with another animal was when I acquired the camel Tulsa from the Tulsa Zoo in Oklahoma. During my horse show at the Wild Animal Park our horses were frequently exposed to other wild animals, but we never did actually work them together. I had seen ponies and camels worked together in the ring, and camels tied on a picket line with horses at the circus, so I decided I wanted to work one of my horses with the camel. By ponying the camel with a horse, I could not only exercise her, but train her to lead better. I decided to use Leo, my black Quarter Horse stallion, who had become acquainted with camels during his circus days. He also had a good temperament around other animals.

I began the introduction by tying the camel to a hitching post and walking the horse up to her. When they became accustomed to one another, I saddled Leo and dallied (wrapped) Tulsa's lead around the horn of the saddle. Next, I put some grain in my pocket, climbed into the saddle, and called for some ground support from my secretary, Cyndee Horn. Until the horse got used to the drag of the camel, and the camel learned her position, I used a slow walk. Each time the camel lagged behind stubbornly, Cyndee would encourage her forward by snapping a whip at her heels. When Tulsa came up beside the horse, I would reward her with grain. We worked in a fenced pasture so that the camel could be contained if she got loose. Whenever Tulsa became upset or frustrated she would bawl like a calf. Leo, though patient, would become irritated when the camel got close to his face. He would pin his ears and snap at her, and she would back up into position beside me looking for reassurance. I found myself acting as mediator between them. Actually, Leo helped keep Tulsa back where I could control her more easily. When she got in front of Leo and it was difficult to control her, we would have to circle away from her, pulling her back into position. When we progressed to a consistent walk, we moved on to a jog, then a lope. We had trouble when we progressed from a jog to a lope because, when a camel runs, it throws its legs in all directions.

Gerri the pig, bred by Joan, shows by comparison just how small Lad is.

As Tulsa ran, she would lift her front legs and hit Leo's hindquarters with her feet. This would cause Leo to crow-hop, or buck. If he got irritable enough, he would kick at her and she would pull back, making it difficult to keep control of both of them. Once they became more accustomed to each other, it was great fun loping for miles across the sandy river bottom. We drew many inquisitive second looks from passersby. At the rate Tulsa is growing, she will soon tower over Leo, so I'm glad we started while she was young.

Here, Letty is being introduced to Devi, a Ceylonese elephant who Joan also trains.

Although zebras are equines, they are not always perceived as such by domestic horses. Since Zelda and Letty have grown up on the ranch they have come to be accepted by our horses, but new arrivals often stop in their tracks upon sighting their first zebra. Such was the case of Cass Ole, the beautiful black Arabian stallion who was the protagonist of the movie *The Black Stallion*. Cass Ole had traveled the country and worked under all possible conditions, but he had never before seen a zebra and wasn't about to trust one.

In the beginning Tulsa was skeptical of Leo.

After a number of training sessions Joan was able to lead Tulsa from horseback.

64

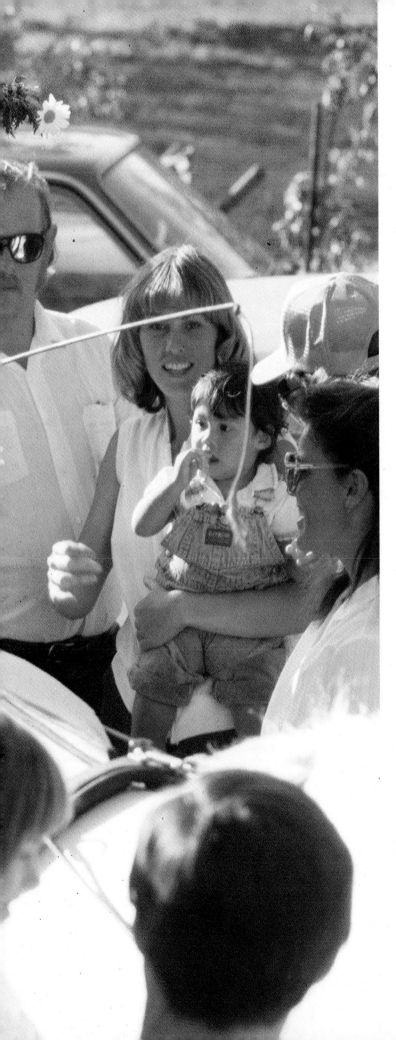

# PARADES

My first experience with animals in a parade was when I took an elephant named Carol from the zoo to the Coronado Fourth of July parade. As the parade began, bands struck up, flags twirled, and entries moved into position. Carol became uneasy with all the commotion. When the antique car behind us tooted its unfamiliar horn, it was the last straw. She took off running, with me on her back, plowing through a couple of fences and a hedge. She was headed for the side of a house when her foot caught in an extendable ladder lying on the lawn. Had she not fallen and come to her senses, I think she would have run right into the house. Then I realized just how hazardous animals could be under parade conditions.

The parade atmosphere takes a special animal. Paraders like exciting horses that people will love to watch, but temperament and training are equally important. The preferable animal is one that is flashy, but controllable under pressure.

There is a great deal of potential for problems at parades. Street surfaces are usually asphalt, which can be slippery for a horse. If it rains, footing can be treacherous, especially for a horse that is shod. Parade spectators are often curious and may not have any knowledge of animals. It's wise to be continually on guard for children who run up unexpectedly and people who place themselves in a vulnerable position, since most are unaware of the potential danger of a frightened animal. This situation can be complicated by parade factors that are uncontrollable. A participating animal could end up behind a band, flag corps, other animals, clowns, motorcycles, or a funny car with a strange horn. It is also not unusual to be near firecrackers, loose balloons, and decorations of all sorts. Traffic, though controlled on the parade, can be heavy in the preparation and dispersal areas, with cars zipping by in all directions.

Since that first parade with the elephant, I've been in many. I've driven carriages, ridden sidesaddle, ponied a camel on horseback, and led a zebra. One factor is common to all parades: They entail a great deal of work. For the fifteen to thirty minutes of glory riding down the street waving to people, it is often necessary to put in two days of preparation. Horses are clipped and bathed, tack cleaned,

One of Joan's duties is to represent the zoo in parades. Here, she drives Finally.

Riding Leo, her Quarter Horse stallion, Joan leads her camel Tulsa.

silver polished, carriage paint retouched, and decorations and costumes readied. Keeping animals clean can be a job in itself. Frequently, parades take place in the morning, so there isn't time to give the animals a complete bath the day of the event. To keep the horses clean, they are bathed the day before, blanketed, and their legs and tails are wrapped. The stalls are carefully cleaned. The trailer is hooked up and all equipment loaded.

The morning of the parade is always hectic with last-minute preparations. Once you arrive at the parade, you are surrounded by curious spectators who want to pet and feed the animals, or just get a closer look or ask questions. It can be difficult to concentrate on what you are doing and supervise at the same time. In many parades the entrant assumes liability.

You must be aware of the potential dangers and do your best to be prepared. There are many things to consider—how many people do you need to help? How close can the public get to the animals without endangering either of them? People can get hurt by doing something unknowingly, so it's your job to look out for them. Someone might walk up to the zebra and pat it on the hindquarters, not realizing she could break their leg with one swift kick. Animals have good days and bad days. Some days they'll accept anything and other days the slightest thing will set them off. They may be tired or irritable.

I find myself evaluating the situation even while I'm grooming the animals and getting ready to go. I may mount my horse and dally the camel's lead rope to the saddle as we move into position, but if I have problems that present a danger to the animals or spectators, I may choose to leave the camel behind or have someone lead it from the ground. The first time we took the zebra and the horse, we had two people on the ground whose only job was to be there in case something unexpected happened.

Pacing in a parade is important because the speed at which you move is determined by what you follow. Stops are frequent. The zebras are a challenge because they balk at unfamiliar sights. To keep them moving, one handler leads, offering treats, and another follows behind to encourage them. When I ride Leo, my black Quarter Horse stallion, I stay behind the zebras so that when they slow or stop, I can ride up behind them to move them forward. They are always wonderful attention getters.

On the other hand, Doc, our Percheron, would rather not wait on anyone. His idea of work is to get on with the show. He has no patience for standing and will bounce up and down when he is stopped for long. Once on the parade route, you are surrounded by spectators on both sides and entries in front of and behind you. There isn't much room to move, especially if you are driving a carriage. You can have your hands full when a horse wants to move out and there's nowhere to go. Patience is a definite attribute.

Weather cannot always be predicted for a parade date and, since they are planned up to a year in advance, most take place rain or shine. I remember spending weeks preparing for the largest parade in San Diego—the Mother Goose Parade. We purchased fresh chrysanthemums, matching ribbons, repainted our antique flower cart, polished the harness, and groomed Melody, our Clydesdale mare, to perfection. We rose early the morning of the parade to a torrential downpour. We waited as long as we could, but it just wouldn't stop raining. Wearing raincoats and rubber boots, we loaded Melody, covered in a blanket and hood, and tried our best to save her beautiful white feathers (the long white hair that grows almost from the Clydesdale's knees to its hooves) by trying between downpours to avoid the numerous mud puddles. It was impossible to keep dry. Once loaded we moved to the parade grounds, then waited in the truck for the weather to clear. Just as it came time to decide whether to go or pull out, it began to clear. After so much

work we decided to try hooking up, though there was a light drizzle. As the parade began, thirty minutes later, the weather cleared and spectators gathered. Unfortunately, many of the horse entries decided it was just too wet and cold, and withdrew at the last minute. It had not been easy to get ready in the pouring rain.

For one year's Christmas parade, I wore a bright red Western suit and rode Leo. We had been teaching the camel to pony with Leo, so I decided to take her along. While we were waiting for the parade to begin the camel became impatient. Each time she tried to move ahead of the horse he'd nip at her and she'd back off. Finally, she became so irritable that when he nipped one more time, she turned and spit all over Leo and me. We had been waiting for an hour, but just as she spit we were called into position. We were then running down the street to catch up while I was trying to wipe off the green mess from my hat, suit, and the horse.

Having a zebra or camel in a parade can frighten other horses, who may have never seen striped or humped beasts. Meanwhile, it is necessary to remember when I pony the camel that she can kick out six feet in any direction, and I have to keep her from getting too close to the spectators. I may be waving and smiling, but I must concentrate completely on what I am doing and, more important, what the animals are doing. It's work!

There have been occasions in parades when control was lost resulting in accidents and injuries. It's frightening when you see it because you know it could happen to you. There was an incident in San Diego last year when a team of horses ran away and could not be stopped by their driver. The driver of an antique car valued at $100,000 tried to stop the runaways by pulling in front of them, but they ran right over the car. Ten people were injured, the car was totaled, and the horses were also injured. It was presumed that fireworks had frightened them.

My most embarrassing moment in a parade occurred when I appeared with Leo and the camel. As I passed the reviewing stand I was introduced as an expert animal handler from the San Diego Zoo. I reached up to wave, and as I did so the camel jerked back, pulling her dallied lead off the saddle horn. She took off running down the street ahead of me. I loped after her and, luckily, a brave bystander grabbed her lead and handed it back to me, or we might have chased her to the end of the parade.

The greatest satisfaction in a parade is watching the children's faces, seeing people become excited about what you've spent so many hours in preparation for. I think there's nothing more exciting than a live animal, whether it is a zebra, a camel, an elephant, or a horse. Few people ever have a chance to be near these animals, so it's special to see them up close, well groomed, and looking their best. If you really love something, you enjoy sharing it with people. You enjoy the fact that other people appreciate it also.

# DRAFT HORSES

The word *draft*, or *draught* (the British spelling), comes from an old English word meaning "pulling." The term draft horse is synonymous with work horse, a horse used for pulling loads. The heavy horse first came into prominence in the Middle Ages, when men wore suits of armor weighing more than two hundred pounds. The knights had shields, as well as swords and lances, and the horses also wore armor. This meant that the animals had to be strong enough to carry immense loads, nearly four hundred pounds. With the invention of gunpowder, however, heavyweight equines in the battlefield proved more of a liability than an asset. Speed became more important than sheer massive weight.

The heavy horse returned to the farm until the need for wagon horses increased when roads were established. Hitched to large wagons, work horses hauled farm produce from rural areas to the cities and raw materials and manufactured goods to and from mills and factories. They were also hitched to barges along canals and rivers.

The importance of draft horses grew as England and other European powers expanded their interests in North America. Land had to be cleared for cultivation, and large horses provided the best means of removing giant boulders, logs, and stumps. Nineteenth-century cities boasted horse-drawn trolley cars, the first means of urban mass transportation. A horse-drawn trolley may be seen today at Disneyland.

The era of the heavy horse was at its peak just prior to World War I. By 1911, the internal combustion engine was beginning to replace horses used for buses, cabs, and vans. The steam engine had been the first mechanical source of power to challenge the horse. Although the railroads took over the transportation of goods for long hauls around the country, they in fact created more work for the heavy horses than they had taken away. There was extensive use of horses by railway companies for short-haul work. During World War I, mainly in America, horses were needed for military purposes, and many farmers had to seek mechanical means to help them achieve the increase in production demanded from the land.

Joan ground drives her Percheron Doc.

The immenseness of the Anheuser-Busch Clydesdales is well demonstrated when they are photographed with Lad.

After the war there was a glut of horses returning from military service. The bottom dropped out of the market for the breeders and many gave up. But by 1925, there was such a shortage of home-bred horses that many were imported from Europe, especially the Percheron breed. By 1960, the draft horse and mule stocks of this country dwindled to the point that they were little known and seldom seen. Three basic groups were responsible for keeping a nucleus of draft-breeding stock alive through those times. Most obvious were the purebred breeders who maintained and propagated heavy horses for show purposes and for use in the big hitches. For the most part, this group was, and is,

made up of prosperous agribusinessmen who kept horses, not because they believed in them as a source of power, but simply because they liked them, enjoyed showing them, and in many cases were carrying on a family tradition of horse breeding.

The Amish in Pennsylvania retained the horse as their only source of motive power and as an integral part of their way of life, both economically and culturally.

Elsewhere, draft horses are fundamental to the economic independence and continuity of the small family farm. In recent years, as the enthusiasm for the draft horse has continued to grow, more heavy horses have been used on small farms and seen in the show ring.

I first became personally involved with draft horses when I took over the ''Show of Horses'' at the Wild Animal Park. There were only a few animals left from the original show, and Melody, a Clydesdale mare, had been purchased as an example of a draft breed. She was easygoing, calm, and everyone got along with her. The most impressive things about Melody were her size and her long, feathered legs. Of all the horses in the show, Melody received the most attention. The audience loved her, probably because of all the popularity of the spectacular Anheuser-Busch horses. She was a pleasure to work with, and it was nice to have a horse in the show that you never had to worry about. She would go anywhere and do anything you asked her to do. She never hurt anybody or caused trouble, as some of the more excitable breeds did. When the horse show closed I hated to see such a good-dispositioned, beautiful mare be sold, so I convinced my supervisors that she should be displayed somewhere in the park. Finally, it was decided that she would be sent to the zoo and displayed in the barnyard exhibit in the Children's Zoo. There she became a very popular exhibit, although there was little space in which to exercise her. When it was decided to remodel the barn and there was no longer room for Melody, I offered to bring her to our ranch. At that point I became even more attached to her. I later purchased her and she became part of our ranch collection.

When we first brought Melody home from the zoo to the ranch, she didn't quite know what to do. She had been in such a small area at the zoo that she seemed mystified when we let her out in the pasture, so much that she stumbled and tripped over her own feet when she tried to run and enjoy the freedom. It was amusing to watch this huge horse lumbering along and trying to gather her legs under her, like a young dog whose feet seem too big and clumsy. Eventually, however, she became much more coordinated. Melody has gone on to become an undefeated Champion Pleasure Riding horse two years in a row at the Los Angeles County Fair Draft Horse Show, competing against many different breeds of draft horses. The Clydesdale breed has often been called the gentle giant, and that seems to describe Melody appropriately. In all the time I've been around her, both here and at the zoo, I've never really gotten over her magnificent size. When I walk up to her she towers over me.

We have great fun with Melody and the carriages and wagons we have acquired. We first bought the carriages to use with Finally, but we soon found that Melody could pull more people, more weight, and was easier to drive because she was so calm. Initially, we used Melody to pull our four-wheeled cart made for light horses, but after going to our first show where we planned to show her in a single driving class, we realized that draft horses have their own type of

vehicle and we didn't have the correct equipment. At that point we started looking for a wagon and a cart for Melody. The first piece of driving equipment we purchased was a freight wagon, which we found to be ideal for transporting people on long picnic rides and hayrides. We could also haul things in the back of the wagon and, most important, for the first time, Melody was being used as a work horse. In the majority of the draft-horse shows, the exhibitors use a two-wheeled cart for single driving, so as soon as we could we purchased one. This enabled Melody to step out and show her action better than with the heavier carriage. Of our draft horses, Melody is the old standby; we can take her anywhere—downtown, through heavy traffic, in parades with firecrackers and lots of people and children—and she never seems to get excited.

Through Melody I became more interested in draft horses and began to look for them at fairs and horse shows. At these events I met Stan and Martha Pilegard, who raise and exhibit Percherons. I fell in love with two of their geldings, Bob and Doc, and I was finally able to purchase them with the first installment from my television series, *The Animal Express.*

Bob and Doc were show hitch horses when we purchased them. They were hotter-tempered, stronger, and tougher to handle than Melody. Of the two, Doc was more difficult to work and really depended on Bob to keep him calm. These horses had what is called a head-up look about them; when working they held their heads up, they moved with snappy leg movement, were always alert, and worked well as a pair. Even when they weren't hitched up together, but just out running loose in their pasture, they were lovely to watch, as even their legs moved in step with one another.

One of the most difficult experiences we've ever had in the horse business was losing one of these two horses that we had literally begged and borrowed money to buy.

As time passed we had begun to really get a feel for the pair, enjoying them by driving them frequently. When Disneyland asked to lease our draft horses for use in their Christmas parade, we thought how exciting it would be not only to watch them in the parade, but how wonderful it would be to share them with all of the Disneyland visitors.

It was the day before Christmas when we received a phone call telling us that Bob was down with colic, he was seriously ill, and the Disneyland veterinarian wasn't sure he was going to survive. For two days he was sick, and every time the phone rang I wondered if it was Disneyland calling to tell me that our horse had died. We had worked very hard to buy him and Doc, and they were so wonderful to have and to drive, we were terribly upset. Finally, the phone rang and we were told that Bob was better, so much so that they were beginning to work him a little. I was ecstatic. To have been so close and not lose this horse—I had seldom been so happy.

When the horses returned from Disneyland we began

driving them and everything seemed to be going well. Then, one night as we were getting ready to go to bed, we heard banging in the barn and Duane rushed out to see what it was. When he returned he said that Bob was so sick that he was down on his side thrashing around, and covered in a sweat. I phoned the animal hospital and was referred to the on-call veterinarian who seemed annoyed at having been woken up. He wanted to know if the horse was really sick enough to warrant a visit to the ranch. It was obvious that Bob was in serious trouble. Duane and I tried to control him as he rolled and thrashed about violently. I then called my personal veterinarian who suggested that we give Bob 40 cc of Dipyrone, a muscle relaxant, and wait to see if that stabilized him. Though 40 cc was a very heavy dose, it had very little effect on the horse. After midnight I again called my veterinarian, and he arrived at the house within minutes. At that point the horse was beginning to go into shock, and was rolling about so violently that we felt he might injure himself, so the veterinarian administered a stronger narcotic. At the time he administered the drug, the veterinarian wasn't sure what condition the horse was in and wondered if the dose was possibly so large that it might kill him right there. After doing his best to sedate Bob and help him, the veterinarian handed us some drugs and told us that we should consider the possibility of having to put the horse down. He was sure he was suffering from a twisted intestine.

Since Bob had survived his two-day bout with colic at Disneyland, we were optimistic about his chances for survival. Then, we decided to try walking him; however, unfortunately, he progressively became worse. It was a cold winter night, and as it began to rain, Duane and I took shifts walking Bob. We would take breaks just to try and get warm. At one point we put the horse in the bullpen, and he rolled and put his foot right through the plywood sides. He was in so much pain, he really didn't have any control over what he was doing. It was then that we began to try to decide whether we should just put him down. At about four or five in the morning he finally went down and didn't get up. The sun was just coming up. Bob took a couple of deep breaths, convulsed, and stopped breathing. It was so sad to see such a powerful and large animal lying there so still. In the soft rain we stood and cried before finally calling the veterinarian.

When the veterinarian did his postmortem, he found that Bob did have a twisted intestine and said there was really no way he could have survived. Before Bob's body was removed I took Doc over to him, thinking he might somehow sense that his friend had died. We thought that by doing so he might be less upset by the separation. You never know what a horse really understands. During the next few days Doc appeared so listless that we put him in the pasture with

Joan and Duane make ranch rounds in the farm wagon.

Melody. But he never really developed the kind of relationship with her that he had had with the Percheron he had grown up with and worked with for so long. He seemed to like Melody's company, but he would chase her off when it came time to eat.

When we first purchased Bob and Doc they were almost inseparable—they walked together, ate together, slept together, and did everything as if they were in harness. And when we lost Bob, it was obviously hard on Doc since he really didn't know what to do without his constant companion. While they were both alive, if we separated them, Doc was always hard to handle; he'd become very impatient and stamp his feet and whinny while trying to move about. He would have attempted anything to be reunited with his friend.

Now we are having a difficult time trying to replace the lost horse with an animal that will match the surviving member of the team. A matched pair must be of the same height, color, size, conformation, and have a similar stride. Aside from the problem of attempting to replace a member of a matched driving pair, we also found that Doc didn't like to be driven alone—he had not only driven with Bob for six years, but they had spent all their time together since they were two or three years old. We began to teach Doc to work alone—ground driving, putting him in between the shafts (something that a horse driven as a pair would not have to do)—and he was eventually able to pull a cart quite nicely by himself. In the past he had had a tendency to hedge a little and let his partner pull harder while he sort of eased back and relaxed. Now, Doc likes to get right down to business when he works, and he becomes impatient with lots of stopping and starting and, for that reason, when we participate in parades, if possible, we use Melody.

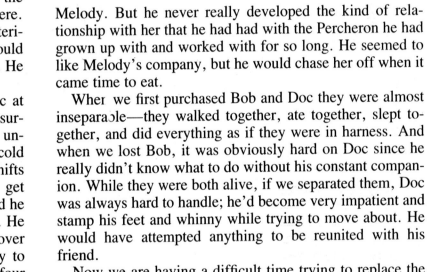

The long white hair, or feathers, of the Clydesdale's legs must be continually groomed to keep them showy.

# MINIATURE HORSES

In the selective-breeding process over many centuries, more than sixty breeds of horses have been developed. Speed, beauty, color, and aptitude for performance are just a few of the characteristics that have been stressed in various breeds. However, in its most exaggerated form, the results of selective breeding in equines can most clearly be seen in the extremes of size—between miniature horses and draft horses. According to the *Guinness Book of World Records,* the largest horse recorded was a Percheron-Shire cross that stood seven feet one inch tall (21.1 hands) and weighed 2,976 pounds. The smallest was a miniature horse standing eighteen inches tall. A draft horse foal at birth is larger than a mature miniature horse.

People who are interested in horses are fascinated by the miniature horse. For many they appear to be the ideal pet— less expensive to maintain than the average horse, yet having the same appeal. They don't require as much space, or eat as much, and because of their size are easier to control. The foals are hard to resist, when you can pick one up and hold its warm, furry little body in your arms. I remember my first visit to a miniature-horse ranch. I was looking for a representative of the breed for my horse show at the Wild Animal Park. We had been shown quite a few animals when I spotted an adorable foal that was the smallest horse I had ever seen. His winter coat was long and shaggy and he looked more like a stuffed toy than a real horse. I bent over to pick him up and as he lay in my lap I knew I had to have him.

As soon as he could be weaned I brought him home. Because we were experiencing unusually cold weather and heavy rains, I decided it would be best to keep him in the house until the weather improved. I had a laundry room with a linoleum floor, which I converted into his bedroom. I named him Atlas and he soon became part of the family. Even the dogs accepted him. He had his own dish next to theirs, but his was filled with alfalfa. During the day Atlas would follow me around the house, and when I sat down he would lean against me with his head resting on my lap. In the evening when friends gathered around the fireplace, Atlas would curl up on the carpet at our feet to sleep. With regular trips outdoors he became fairly well housebroken.

Ultra Story, a day-old miniature foal

Joan towers over the day-old foal.

One of my favorite photographs is of Atlas lying on my bed watching himself on the television screen while he appeared on the *Tonight* show. We had taped the show with Atlas at five-thirty that evening. Having come straight home from NBC studios, we were able to watch the show air at eleven-thirty that same night.

Atlas rode in the cab of my pickup truck, standing on the floor with his head resting on the seat. I took him everywhere and he seemed to enjoy the outings. When he was strong enough I moved him to the park, where he became a favorite attraction. He was our mascot and he regularly ate lunch with us in the tack room.

A few years later I acquired my first own miniature horse. I had received a call from the office of Colonel Parker, the agent for Elvis Presley. He wanted to donate three miniature horses to the zoo, one stallion and two mares. The stallion went to the zoo, one mare to the Wild Animal Park, and the second mare I purchased from the zoo. I found a small registered black stallion to breed her to and she produced a black colt. I then bought a thirty-two-inch chestnut stallion and named him Lakeside Lad. He has appeared on many television shows, such as *Merv Griffin, Mike Douglas,* the

Because of their size, miniature horses cannot be ridden, but they can be driven.

Joan and her niece with a miniature foal filly

*Tonight* show, and the *John Davidson Show*. Lad can lie down, sit, salute, march, bow, and walk on his hind legs on cue. He travels to parades, lectures, and promotions of all kinds. It is much easier to transport him and maneuver him in and out of tight spots than larger horses or wild animals. He is always a crowd pleaser, with his proud prancing gait, long flowing mane, and tail that drags on the ground. Despite his small size, he seems to always have a "Hey! Look at me!" attitude.

According to the International Miniature Horse Registry, the miniature horse was first bred in the royal courts of Europe during the seventeenth century. Selectively bred by crossing the smallest horses, they became prized possessions in the royal stables, often pets of princes and princesses. As the extravagant courts of Europe disappeared, the miniature horses found their way into traveling circuses and were scattered around the world.

The first of these animals imported to the United States from Europe in the 1930s were used in the coal mines. They hauled coal cars up the narrow shafts that were too small for horses and mules. In the 1960s the Regina Winery imported a herd from the famous Falabella Ranch in Argentina. The miniatures bred on this ranch became foundation stock for the Falabella Miniature Horse Registry. These miniatures were later sold to breeders in this country. In part due to all the attention they received from the press, the miniature gained recognition, and in the 1970s became very popular in the United States. Since that time they have become increasingly popular, with more and more recognized shows being offered specifically for them. These shows have undoubtedly contributed to raising the standards by which these lilliputians are judged and bred.

To be registered, a miniature cannot exceed a height of thirty-four inches when fully grown. The height is deter-

mined by measuring the vertical distance from the base of the mane (at the withers) to the ground. Foals are given temporary papers until their third year, at which time the owner can apply for permanent registration if the size requirements are met. The two most active registries in the United States are the International Miniature Horse Registry and the American Miniature Horse Association. In competition, miniature horses are judged not just for size, but for correct conformation as well. The only performance class in which they compete is driving. Although they may only be ridden by extremely small children, they can make good cart horses.

Miniature horses come in various colors and types. Choosing one can be difficult, but once you have it, it is sure to win your heart.

Nowhere is the diversity of domestic equines more obvious than in the comparison of the miniature horse to the draft horse.

# SHOEING

With the domestication of the horse, man became increasingly responsible for providing food, shelter, medical care, and hoof care. Although wild equines manage without shoes, they live a different life-style from their captive relatives.

Horses doing heavy work require shoes to protect their hooves from excessive wear. Obviously, the conditions under which the horse is used determine its hoof-care needs. Horses used in sandy or soft soil may never need shoes, although they will require regular trimming; while those used in rocky country will need shoes for even a small amount of use. Others standing idle may have excessive hoof growth.

Aside from preventing too rapid wear of the hoof wall and tenderness and injury to the hoof, shoes are used to provide grip, to change the angle or breakover of the foot, as an aide to healing in case of injury, and to correct or improve faults in the horse's gait. The shape and quality of the hoof is another factor. A large, flat-bottomed hoof will become tender faster than a narrower, more concave foot because the sole is more exposed. Thick-walled, hard hooves may not need shoes under the same conditions that a horse with thin-walled and soft or poor-quality hooves would. Sometimes shoes are used primarily for their decorative effect. A good farrier is able to correct faults of conformation, improve the condition of a horse's feet, and prevent weaknesses from developing. Bad shoeing can lame a horse.

When I was given my first horse, I had to call a farrier to trim his feet regularly. As I watched the man work on Finally, I thought how convenient it would be if I could do it myself. Eventually, I enrolled in a vocational school program that offered a course in horseshoeing. The class met two nights a week and all day Saturday for a whole year. Although I loved horseshoeing, I soon found out there is more to it than first meets the eye. Our goals were to learn how to use a forge, how to make a shoe by hand from a piece of flat bar stock, how to control a horse during the shoeing process, how to trim a foot, how to nail on a shoe, and how to do corrective work. An understanding of the anatomy and physiology of the horse's legs and feet is es-

Joan is one of the few horsewomen who can do their own shoeing.

sential. I soon found out how taxing horseshoeing is physically. I also learned that it really is an art.

Very few people appreciate how much skill and knowledge a farrier must have until they try to do it themselves. It not only necessitates being a good metal worker with diagnostic skills and a special feel for the shape of a hoof, but it also requires a proficiency in handling horses. When we started shoeing, we had to work with the horses that other farriers wouldn't, or horses people took to the shoeing school to get the job done free. Not only did we have to learn how to trim and hold the hoof, but to shape the shoes and control the horse as well. I remember being absolutely terrified that I was going to ''quick'' the horse—cut off too much of his hoof and make it bleed. It is very difficult at first to assume the shoeing position for any length of time. A horse will not hold its foot up in an uncomfortable position. Being tall, I had to bend more to get down under the horse. So, in order to make the animal comfortable, I had to stand hunched over with bent knees. The muscular coordination and conditioning required is more than you can imagine. I remember that I would get to the point where my knees would tremble, my muscles would ache and quiver, and I would be so sore at the end of the day I could barely walk. All I wanted to do was sit down and put up my feet. Most of the horses I learned on were not very manageable, and just about the time I'd get ready to cut, or get my shoe ready to nail, the horse would give me trouble. Then I would be back to square one again.

I found that shaping the shoe was one of the toughest parts of shoeing. I would take a ready-made shoe, place it up against the bottom of the horse's hoof, decide what changes I should make, and then go back to the anvil to pound that shoe into the shape I wanted. I would get the shoe almost right, except for one slight adjustment. I'd go back to the anvil again to fix that problem, and somehow I would get the rest of it out of shape. Then, I would go back to the anvil, back to the hoof, back and forth until I had it right. I remember thinking, ''Hey, this is ridiculous! It takes me eight hours to shoe one horse.'' I realized I would never be able to make a living in the shoeing business, but I did learn enough to be able to appreciate good work, to do my own trimming, to pull shoes, and to nail them on.

It was a memorable day when I finally got my own anvil

Joan finishes a hoof after trimming it.

I have worked on feet as small as those of a miniature horse and on hooves as large as those of a draft horse. If I hold a draft-horse foot, weighing fifty pounds or more, in my lap for any amount of time, I soon find myself dripping with sweat. I try to get the job done as quickly as possible. When I first acquired Melody, she developed a habit of trying to sit on me. Can you imagine a two-thousand-pound horse trying to sit on the person who is holding up her foot? Teaching her to stand on her own three legs involved hours of training. She was just a little lazy. Every time she'd try to sit on me, I'd have to drop her foot and pick it up again. I finally had to discipline her when she began to lean.

After all my hours in class I mastered everything but the shaping of shoes. One of the requirements of shoeing school was to make a horseshoe from flat bar stock. I had to take a piece of flat, straight metal, shape it, punch the holes for the nails in the shoe, and then make a bar shoe by welding the heels of the shoe together in the fire. I don't know how many horseshoes I burned up before I finally got a good weld. It was difficult to heat the shoe sufficiently for welding knowing that only a few degrees more would cause it to disintegrate.

Someday, when I have more time, I would like to perfect my metal-working skills. The shoeing skills I have mastered are invaluable with so many horses on the ranch. It is more convenient and less costly to be able to do much of their hoof care myself.

There are many different styles of shoes designed for particular breeds and types of work.

to go along with my shoeing tools. Anvils are fairly expensive; they cost around $350 to $400, and the tools at least $200. However, it is nice to be able to repair a broken nail, and to shape or correct a hoof whenever I need to. After going through a year of training, I found I was inclined to pay a little more to have a good job done on my own horses, particularly if I was going to be showing them. I would call in a top farrier to shoe them because he could do better work than I could.

I became so interested in the shoeing of horses that I developed quite a collection of shoes. There is a wide variation in styles of shoes for the type of work a horse does. Gaited horses have weighted shoes for more action; race horses wear lightweight aluminum plates for greater speed; jumpers have shoes with heel calks for traction; road horses have barium on the bottom of their shoes for traction, and wear leather or rubber pads to soften the concussion to their hooves. Screw-in calks or spikes give horses traction in ice and snow. There are also shoes to correct foot or gait problems.

# THE THREE-DAY EVENT

E venting first became an Olympic sport at the Stockholm Olympics in 1912. Competition was open only to military officers on active duty—riding military horses as a test of strength, versatility, and endurance of the riders and their mounts. European cavalry officers had developed the sport over many years. It combined dressage, cross-country, and stadium jumping. Each competition was held on a separate day, which gave the sport its name. Dressage showed that the horse was calm, obedient, and precise on the parade ground. Cross-country showed the horse was fit enough and bold enough to cover miles and miles of difficult terrain at speed. Stadium jumping established that the horse, after a grueling day under battle conditions, was still sound enough to continue performing the duties expected of him.

With the removal of equines from the battlefield, eventing became a civilian sport. The 1948 Games in London were the last major performance of the U.S. Army Equestrian Team, which was disbanded in 1949. Women were not permitted to participate in an Olympic three-day event until the 1964 Olympic Games in Tokyo. Previously, dressage and jumping teams had included women competitors, but the three-day sport remained an exclusive male domain. Today, the three-day event has become increasingly popular not only with contestants, but also with spectators. In England it is a major sport. I remember watching Princess Anne riding in an event that was televised and attended by thousands of spectators.

Although the full-scale three-day event as presented in Olympic Games and championship competitions requires three full days, abbreviated forms of it have been gaining popularity. For qualification as a combined-training event, at least two of the three basic phases must be offered. Events may be scheduled with all three tests on one day. Trials are conducted at various levels, from the pre-training level, intended for green horses or novice riders, to the advanced levels in Olympic and national championships. The levels include pre-training, training, preliminary, intermediate, and advanced. With each level of competition, the various tests become increasingly demanding. Dressage tests progress from the very simplest movements to those requiring more and more training and coordination. The required speeds for the cross-country test become faster, the

Eagle is lunged over a fence.

Joan dressed in typical eventing attire

length of the courses longer, and the size of the obstacles larger. A steeplechase is not included below the preliminary level because the physical development and training of the horses have not reached a point where it is advisable to jump obstacles at speed.

Horses are submitted to a veterinary inspection before the start of the competition, again during the speed and endurance test, with a final check before the show-jumping test on the last day. The same horse and rider have to compete in all three tests, and the competitor with the lowest total of penalties is the winner.

Dressage, which can be likened to the school figures in a skating competition, is probably the least understood of the three phases. The word *dressage* means "training" in French. The emphasis in dressage is on the precision of the horse's movements, the degree of control exercised by the rider, and the combined style of man and animal. The top levels of dressage often take as many as seven years of training. A typical dressage test is made up of some twenty movements, each one judged on a scale from zero to ten. Within a set time allowance of seven and a half to fifteen minutes in an arena twenty by sixty meters, the horse performs various gaits (walk, trot, canter) in different forms (natural, collected, extended). These maneuvers must be executed in specific areas marked by large letters placed along the edges of the arena. The exercises and routes to be followed in a dressage test are described in a diagram furnished to each contestant. Most tests are memorized before the rider enters the ring. The entire dressage exhibition asks nothing of the horse that is not natural. It is amazing how

much work is involved in adapting the natural movement of a horse to the complete control of his rider. The panel of judges must consider such qualities as freedom and regularity of paces, impulsion on the part of the horse, attention and obedience, lightness and ease of movement, acceptance of the bit, position and seat of the rider, and correct use of the aids (whips and spurs).

The cross-country ride and steeplechase on the second day is the most physically demanding phase of the three-day event. It covers a distance of up to sixteen miles, with demerits for refusal of a horse to take an obstacle; for a rider's fall, and for failing to complete the course in the prescribed time. Riders start individually, and the test is made up of four phases. The first, roads and tracks, is designed to warm up the horse and rider for the more demanding tests that follow. It is usually from two to four miles in length and must be accomplished within a set time allowance.

The steeplechase is designed to test the horse's ability to jump at speed over ten steeplechase obstacles on a course approximately two miles in length. The course must be ridden within a set time period. Immediately following the steeplechase, the horse continues on a second roads and tracks from six to ten miles in length.

The final element of the second day is the four- to five-mile cross-country course, including twenty to thirty-two fixed obstacles of varied design.

The third phase of the three-day event is stadium jumping. The course is seven hundred to one thousand yards, with ten to twelve obstacles. Penalties are incurred for knockdowns, refusals at the obstacles, and for exceeding the time allowed. This course is not as demanding as a standard show-jumping course, but it is designed to determine whether, after a severe test of speed and endurance, the horse has retained the suppleness, energy, and obedience necessary to continue working.

There is competitive jumping in three basic fields: hunters, jumpers, and combined training. The hunter (developed for cross-country hunts) is judged on conformation, style, way of going, and manners. He should be correctly balanced and a pleasure to ride. The jumper is judged on his athletic ability rather than his conformation. He need not be a pleasure to ride, but he must be able to clear the course within the time allowance. Speed is often a factor in determining the winner. The combined-training horse may not be as competitive as a hunter or jumper, but he should have the stamina, courage, and versatility for the demands of combined training.

My first experience in dressage came through my interest in combined training. Although I had a great deal of riding experience, the precise nature of this discipline made the simplest of movements challenging. If the test calls for a ten-meter circle at B, it means you must begin and end a circle of ten meters in diameter at reference point B. In my first competition I remember being extremely nervous as the

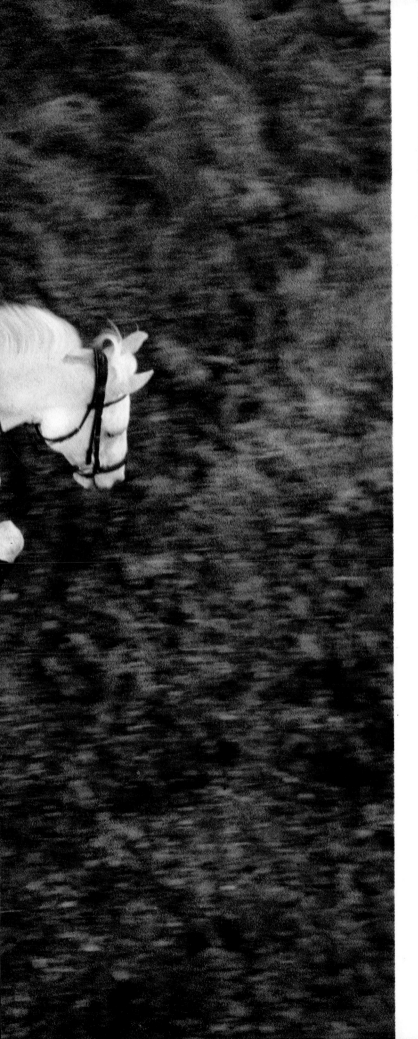

In this series Joan takes a jump on the cross-country course.

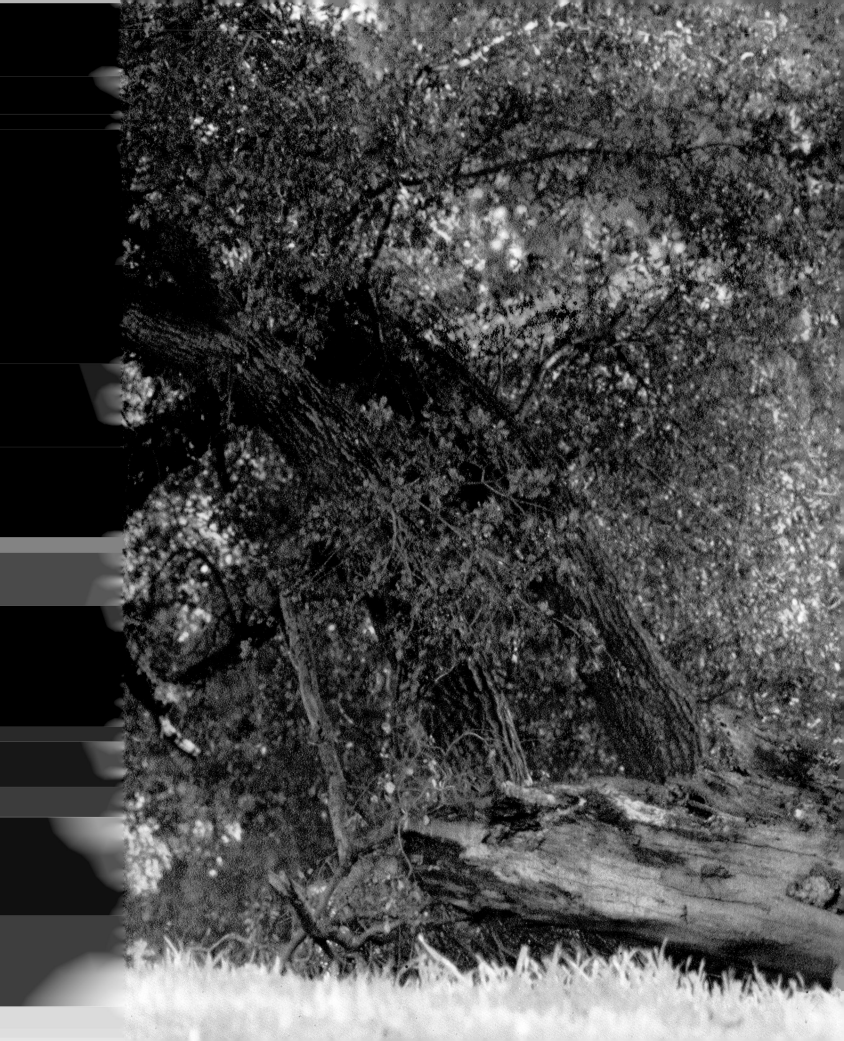

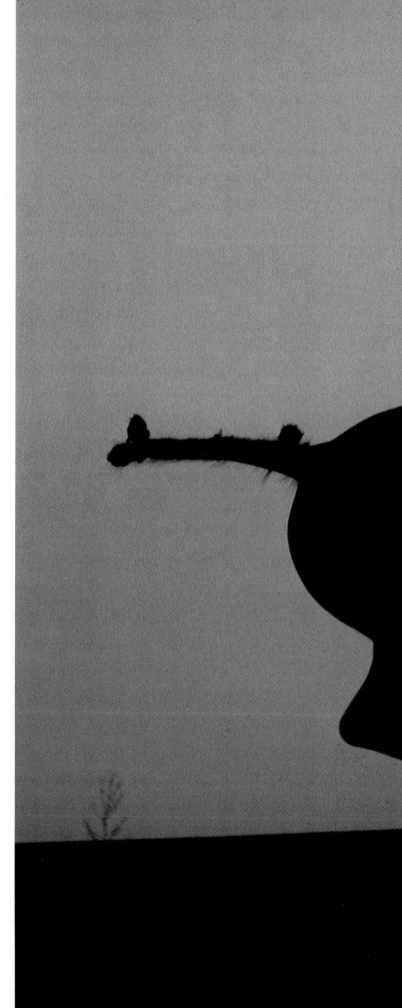

bell rang signaling me to enter the ring. I trotted in to a traditional halt in center arena, followed by a salute to the judge. My stomach sank as I felt her undivided attention on my every move. I was not in a class with fifteen or twenty other horses, as I had been in past shows. Under her scrutiny every minor flaw seemed major. When I finished the test I was hesitant to look at my final score and comments. Fortunately, her opinion of my ride was better than mine, and my score gave me the encouragement to continue.

Having gained some confidence, I set out on the cross-country phase of the event. I made it through the roads and tracks in good time and was on to the cross-country obstacle course. While galloping across the beautiful countryside and clearing the rustic fences in my path, I was beginning to enjoy the thrill of competition. As I galloped up a steep incline, my horse gathered to clear the log fence in front of us. Once airborne I knew we were in trouble. He had stumbled on takeoff and his front feet caught the solid barrier. The world turned upside down as my horse somersaulted completely, head first, and landed on his back. Fortunately, I was thrown clear of the horse. We both lay there momentarily stunned. My whole body ached as I rose to grab the reins and check the horse. I feared he might be seriously

Here, Joan jumps onto and across a one-stride table jump.

injured, but he rose to his feet awkwardly. As I walked him away from the fence, I was relieved to see he seemed to be all right. It is a wonder he didn't break his neck or land on top of me. Slowly, I pulled myself back into the saddle, assuring the approaching spectators I was not hurt. I finished the course cautiously. As I dismounted, I noticed for the first time the deep cuts and scratches on my brand-new saddle, scrapes that hurt more than the ones on my arms and face.

While I was taking riding lessons, I enjoyed watching the jumping. After I had developed some basic riding skills, I signed up for jumping lessons and was given an experienced school horse to ride. It was a good thing he knew what he was doing. In trying to second-guess when the horse was going to jump, I was either forward too early or left behind. I learned how difficult it is to direct a horse when the rider is not properly balanced. Gradually, I developed a feel for the

Joan in required dressage attire

Eagle and Joan going over a stadium jump

horse's movement and progressed from cavallettis, poles on the ground, to higher and more varied obstacles. I began to combine elements until I could work an entire course. Riding many different school horses gave me a feel for adjusting to the style of each. It made me a more flexible rider.

Gradually, I prepared for my first show, a "hunter's over fences" class. I was very nervous, so much I could hardly think straight. Each rider must memorize a specific predetermined course before he enters the ring. Once on course the rider may not circle or cross his tracks. I entered the arena, put my horse into a canter, and headed for my first fence in competition. I was thinking only of that fence, which was cleared with ease. I was relieved momentarily, until I realized my mind had gone blank and I had no idea where I was headed. Panicked, I circled and was immediately eliminated for being off-course before I even got over my second fence. I was tremendously embarrassed, and I have never again forgotten to always be looking for the next fence.

Jumping requires athletic ability, coordination, and courage on the part of both horse and rider. The horse must be powerful and yet controllable, and the rider has to acknowledge there is a certain amount of risk involved. In all my years of working with wild animals and horses, most of my injuries have been related to jumping. The thrill of jumping is a feeling of power as more than a thousand pounds of horse comes up underneath you in that moment of being airborne; and the horse has the athletic ability to collect himself and go on to the next fence.

Eagle in a half-pass

# LIBERTY

Whenever the circus came to town, I remember being fascinated by Liberty horses decorated with beautiful plumes and shiny patent leather harness dancing to music. The feeling of majesty that comes from watching them in action is the result of seeing animals free, yet with grace and precision following the slightest cue from their handler. Liberty horses are so called because they work at liberty without a rider or rein. The horses respond to cues from the trainer's body position in the ring and the position of the whip (which is used to direct them).

My first opportunity to venture beyond being a Liberty act spectator came when the zoo hired a new trainer, Don McLennan, who had for many years trained circus horses. We found an immediate mutual love for horses, and when our zoo training was done he invited me to his home to see some Liberty horses he was training. It looked so easy as he put them through their paces. When he offered to let me give it a try, I jumped at the opportunity.

Once in the ring the horses were immediately on guard. Don gave me instructions on how to cue each movement, but it seemed I was always in the wrong spot. In the ring every move a human makes is perceived by the horses to be some kind of cue. If the horses become confused, which they often are with a new person in the ring, they make mistakes. With more than one animal in the ring, when one horse makes a mistake, it throws the others off. It seems that one mistake leads to another. Even more frustrating for me was the fact that Don was able to go into the ring and immediately remedy the situation. I soon found out it wasn't as easy as it looked. Every trainer has his own style, but the horses always work best for the trainer who broke them. Eventually, however, the horses will develop confidence in a new trainer.

Liberty horses are each trained separately, then gradually introduced into a group. The lead horse should be confident and ready to take direction. Each horse has a specific position in the group, which he learns. If one gets out of position, he must be able to find his place again. It's interesting to watch horses make room for another to get back into position, or to see them pin their ears and kick at the one who is out of place.

Joan with her Liberty team in show harness

To control the horse during the first stages of training, he is put on a lungeline so that he can be positioned by the trainer. If at any time during training control is lost, the horse is returned to the lungeline. As the horses are introduced to a group, each is on a separate lungeline. Gradually, the lines are dropped and the horses are at Liberty. The cues they watch for include the position of the handler in the ring, the position of the whip, and the use of the voice. Inconsistency of any of these cues will confuse the horses. The key to working animals for Liberty is to keep calm and be distinct in giving cues so that they will not become confused. Some people think of a whip as being cruel, but a horse that has been mistreated with a whip will be so frightened of it he cannot respond properly. The horse should watch the position of the whip for a cue, but not be frightened of it. The tone of voice can have a calming effect or be used to get the horse's attention, depending how it is used. Body position can be used to slow a horse down or speed him up, to move him out to the rail or bring him in to the center of the ring. It can also cue a waltz, change direction, or line up the horses. Combinations of cues are frequently used, but well-schooled horses often respond from either the body alone or just the whip.

My first attempts at Liberty training were with Finally when he was still too young to be ridden. He seemed to look forward to the training sessions as another form of attention. We were both so proud of our newfound skills, I would spend hours perfecting each move and relate each day's progress or problems to Don.

The first order of work begins on the lungeline as the horse learns to lunge in a circular ring about forty feet to fifty feet in diameter, slowing or increasing his pace on command. He then learns to change direction by circling in toward the center of the ring, then back out the other direction. To cue this the trainer steps toward the rail in the direction the horses are moving, thereby cutting them off. They will move to the inside of the ring, and as they do the trainer follows them back to the rail with his whip. A series of consecutive changes makes a figure eight pattern.

Each horse must be whip broke to come to the trainer when called. This is trained in a small corral or stall where the horse is within range of the whip. He is called to the trainer by name and rewarded each time he moves toward the trainer. If he turns away he is flicked on the haunches until he turns toward the trainer, at which time he is rewarded. As the animal is called, the trainer steps back and encourages him to come forward by flicking the whip on the haunches. Once a horse is whip broke he can be called to the center of the ring or called out of the line. Each member of the group can be positioned separately, then moved back into his place. Turnbacks demonstrate how horses can be removed from the line. First the last animal is called in, then turned back to move in the direction opposite that of the other horses. Then he can be called in again, then turned back to find his place in line. Next, two horses can be turned back in the opposite direction and again returned to their places in line. The cue to call a horse in is to step back and drop the whip.

A waltz is trained by bringing a horse in, then moving him back to the rail in a circular fashion, so that he is pivoting on his haunches 360 degrees to return to the direction he was originally going. This can be trained by wrapping a lungeline around the horse's neck so that as he comes in, his head can be turned back to the rail again. The cue is to step

*(Top row)* Joan's three horses move into a "wheel."

*(Bottom row)* Jason, the third horse, is turned back to move in the opposite direction of the other two animals.

*(Top row)* Joan turns back the last two horses to move in the opposite direction.
*(Bottom row)* Joan "waltzes" the three horses simultaneously.

back, then forward in order to push the horse's head back to the rail again. The challenge is to get all horses waltzing in unison. Pairs can be taught to waltz head to tail. A wheel is performed when all horses line up horizontally to the trainer side by side. This is cued when the trainer turns his body from facing the horses to positioning himself sideways to them. They can again be returned to the rail if the trainer changes his body position to face the animals while moving them back out with the whip.

After my horses perform each of these basic movements, they are called into the center ring. Two wooden pedestals are placed at opposite ends of the ring and the horses are once again sent out to the rail. They are then made to circle the ring, after which the last horse is cued to place his front feet on a pedestal. As the other two horses move on around the ring, the second horse is then cued to stand on the opposite pedestal. The third horse then changes direction in a figure eight around the animals on pedestals. He finishes the routine by coming to the center to take a bow.

To train a horse to get on a pedestal, he is first led up to it and a front foot is picked up by the trainer and placed on the pedestal. Then the animal is rewarded and encouraged to place both front feet on the pedestal. The bow can be trained by pulling a leadrope between the horse's front legs while with a reward (carrot, apple, grain), its head is enticed down between its legs until its face is horizontal to the ground. Each time the animal finds the correct position a cue (tap on the shoulder) is given simultaneously, so that when the horse is free, he will respond to the cue alone.

The last behavior trained is the rear. It is important to use a great deal of caution with this behavior because it can easily become an undesirable vice. When a horse is show-

ing resistance, he soon finds the rear an easy defense mechanism. The rear is trained by encouraging the horse to lift his front feet off the ground, then gradually working for more height. A whip-broke horse will learn to walk forward in the rearing position, which is called a hind leg walk.

One day in the winter of 1981, we received a call from Don McLennan, who was in town with the circus with which he was traveling. When we went to visit him and see his Liberty and high school acts, we were able to enjoy a wonderful behind-the-scenes look at circus life.

The next day the circus was again on the road; however, we were shocked to learn that Don had suffered a heart attack and was in serious condition in the hospital. We offered to pick up his horses and keep them at the ranch until he was well. After Don had been released from the hospital, he spent a week at the ranch recuperating. Since he would no longer be able to travel, he decided to sell the horses

Joan figure eights the lead horse around two horses on tubs.

Joan with her three Liberty horses, Gallo, Diamond, and Jason

My first experience working the horses away from the ranch was at the Aid to Zoos Horse Show in Phoenix, Arizona, which is held in an indoor coliseum and, with over seven hundred entries, is one of the largest horse shows in the Western states. This experience was quite overwhelming for me and for my horses, who had not been off the ranch for several years. They had to work indoors, under lights, with an audience, music, announcer, and other horses nearby. Because of the show's busy schedule there wasn't time for a practice. At each performance I was given a remote microphone to introduce the horses and explain the demonstration. I was so nervous my mouth was dry as I began to speak. ''My lead horse Diamond is a half-Lipizzan, half-Arabian gelding. Siglavy, my second horse, is a Lipizzan stallion, and the third horse, Jason, is an Arabian gelding.''

The horses were wild-eyed taking in everything they saw. It was like trying to keep calm three kids suffering from stage fright. I felt even more nervous than usual knowing I was surrounded by top horse trainers and riders. As the routine began I cued the change of direction and took a deep breath when all three horses responded correctly. As I executed a series of changes the audience applauded and, gaining confidence, I cued for turnbacks. Being nervous, the horses were moving faster than usual and it was tricky getting them positioned. Next came the waltz. As I gave the cue, Diamond and Siglavy pivoted to the music, but Jason seemed to be in another world. I tried again to get all three horses to waltz simultaneously, but when Jason cantered past the other two horses, the crowd rocked with laughter. To get Jason's attention I snapped my whip at him, but it was Siglavy, more sensitive than Jason, who responded. The other two horses sensed something was wrong. To avoid exciting them more I went on with the rest of the routine. What a tremendous relief it was when Diamond took his final bow and we finished that first performance. To my surprise everyone enjoyed the show; people particularly liked Jason—the independent one! The performances improved each day as the horses became more familiar with their surroundings. Though we never achieved a completely perfect performance, I knew that it was possible to do so and that we had come close.

I enjoy working Liberty horses; however, I don't think circus life is for me. My one experience traveling with a circus, in England, taught me that life under the big top is not all glamour, but hard work and long hours. Mary Chipperfield, with whom I traveled, was up each morning at the crack of dawn to practice her routines. After lunch it was time to get dressed for the afternoon performance, followed a few hours later by the evening performance. Every few days the tent would come down after the last show and the circus would move to another town. For those moments of glamour in the ring, the circus is a never-ending series of responsibilities.

rather than haul them back to Oregon, where he lived. During the week with us he had shown me how to work the act, and I was having such a good time I finally decided to buy the three animals myself. Each day until he left Don would watch me work, correcting my mistakes; however, when he left for Oregon I wondered how the horses would behave when I was on my own.

Whenever visitors came to see my animals I would work the Liberty horses, and on several occasions they performed for television shows taped at the ranch. On my television series, *The Animal Express*, I showed John Ritter of *Three's Company* how to work Liberty. It was amusing to watch someone else in the same confusing position I had experienced my first time in the ring. But John was a great sport and finally did quite well.

Joan changes the horses' direction.

# CUTTING

Cutting horses are unique in the horse world because they work independently of the rider. In fact, in competition the rider is penalized for assisting the horse. My first opportunity to ride a cutting horse came when Jerry Lucas, the trainer on our ranch, let me ride his Quarter Horse stallion, Docs Triple Bar. I was told to take a deep seat, hold on to the saddle horn, and not interfere with the horse once he understood which cow was to be separated from the others. With Jerry's guidance I moved Doc into the herd of cattle. His head and neck dropped into a relaxed position as he seemed to move casually through the herd. While the cattle sifted past us, Jerry pointed to one steer and I guided Doc toward him to try and prevent him from returning to the group. Once the steer was cut from the herd, my work was over and Doc's had just begun. As he lowered his nose facing the steer, his ears and eyes fixed on the animal with intent. Trying to get by the horse, the steer pivoted and ran to one side, but as he did so, Doc spun on his haunches to block him. The steer, not willing to give up, made a series of attempts to pass the horse, but each time the horse cut him off. Doc seemed to know in advance what the steer was going to do, anticipating each move. In expectation, Doc would shift his weight from one front leg to the other. It was quite a challenge, even with all my years of riding, to avoid being left sitting in the dirt or hanging off the side of the saddle as the horse moved explosively under me.

There isn't anything quite like the feeling of riding a good cutting horse. Duane and I both decided it was something we would enjoy learning more about, so we asked Jerry to find us a good horse with which to learn. He found a mare that would not only serve that purpose, but would be a good broodmare as well. We purchased her and I began to take lessons. Blitzann (or Annie as we call her) knew more about cutting than I did. I was a passenger going along for the ride, trying to develop a feel for the moves. Jerry began teaching me the basic positions, what was supposed to happen, and where Annie was supposed to be and when.

It was hard to avoid directing the horse with my hands. I was so used to having full control of the horse I was riding, it was not easy for me to accept the idea of dropping the reins. When I tried to direct Annie, I would often anticipate

Here, Bar De Bye is "locked on" on his cow. His total concentration can be read by his expression.

The extreme athletic ability and catlike movements typify a good cutting horse. Here, Joan and Bar De Bye keep a cow from returning to the herd.

incorrectly which direction the cow was going to move. Annie would ignore me while making the correct move.

It looks so easy when you see a well-trained horse with a good rider. A good horse moves so fast it is impossible to outthink him, so you have to develop a feel for following his movements. I would be in good position on the first turn to block the steer, but as Annie swung back and forth, I would become further and further behind. A top cutting horse will challenge the best of riders.

As a hardworking ranch hand, the cutting horse played a major role in the development of the West. Because of the open ranges, the cow horse became invaluable in the cattle

A good dog can be extremely helpful in working cattle.

industry when animals needed to be separated from the herd for branding, medicating, weaning, or moving to market. Although they developed as work animals, proud boasts by cowboys and challenges backed by money inspired the cutting-horse contests that gained broader recognition through the turn of the century. In 1946, the National Cutting Horse Association formed and placed the event under a uniform set of rules. The annual NCHA futurity is the richest indoor horse event in the world, with over two thousand horses nominated (entered) and over one million dollars in prize money. Today, there are ten thousand members in the NCHA.

Cutting horses are selected for their cow sense—their ability to outthink a cow. Pedigree, conformation, athletic ability, and training are all important factors. In competition a rider is given two-and-a-half minutes to ride into the herd, select an individual cow, and drive it from the herd. The cow has a strong desire to remain with the group and will try to return to the herd by finding a way past the horse. After the rider has made his cut, it is the responsibility of the horse to prevent the cow from returning to the herd. The rider is not allowed to rein the horse once the horse knows which cow has been selected. The horse is judged on his style and athletic ability, how hard he is challenged, and by the mistakes he makes. Any assistance from the rider can be penalized once the cut is made. The rider may signal the horse to stop and re-enter the herd to cut another cow within the allotted time. Each judge (in large competitions there are more than one) scores the horse between sixty and eighty points, with sixty being zero and eighty being perfect. Penalty points are deducted when the cow reaches the back fence (three points) or returns to the herd before the horse is signaled to stop (five points).

There are four assistants: two herd handlers and two turn-back riders. Moving into the herd and working through the cattle is an important part of the horse's work, as it must remain calm enough to keep the cattle from getting excited and scattering. A horse must be very athletic and explosive while working a single cow, but must walk into the herd quietly with its head down, seemingly without a care in the world. On the range, the ability to move into a herd unnoticed was important because a rider could be seriously injured if a herd became restless and stampeded.

There are two terms used most frequently in the cutting-horse business: one is that they have cow, meaning that they have the natural instinct or intuition to work the cow on their own; the other is catlike, when the horse will drop down on its front end face-to-face with a cow and move back and forth from one foot to the other in a ready position, almost as if stepping on eggs, in order to move quickly enough to cut off the cow. You will also hear the term locked-in, meaning that the horse is concentrating only on the cow and oblivious to anything else around him, waiting for even the slightest move that the cow makes to get by.

Joan finds cutting to be one of the most thrilling of equine activities.

Cutting horses are not supposed to show aggression in any way; they are only supposed to hold their position on an imaginary line and not allow the cow to infringe on their space or return to the herd. If the horse moves toward the cow once he begins to work the animal, it is called leaking. They are in a sense guarding a specific space just a little way past where the herd stands, and they must not move too far forward or too far back, which could scatter the entire herd. The horse is not supposed to injure or chase the cow, which might cause it to become overly excited and more difficult to handle, especially if someone should be trying to move it or rope it.

Roping horses are trained to follow a cow in order to help a rider get close enough to rope it, but a cutting horse does not go after a cow. Sometimes a cutting horse will become so frustrated in its desire to have the cow make a move that it will behave aggressively. Such behavior is not desirable. Sometimes the horse will almost try to bait the cow into moving, and will reach down and try to bite it. Frequently, sour cattle—those that have been used so much that they are no longer afraid of the horses—will try to escape by dashing by underneath the horse rather than trying to go around him. This tends to make the horse so angry, he will try to bite a cow in order to get the animal out from under his feet.

Although any horse can learn to cut, most competitive cutting horses are Quarter Horses specifically bred for cattle work. True to the traits for which the Quarter Horse is known, a cutting horse must be compact, very maneuverable, able to move quickly, to sit down on his hocks, and to stop and turn quickly to outmaneuver the cow. Initially, the trainer positions the horse where he will have the best advantage to work the cow correctly. Eventually, the cutting horse will assume the correct position and his innate cow sense will take over. Slower cattle can be used to train inexperienced horses that need to develop confidence, but it is essential to have fresh cattle to tune a good horse. As a horse progresses in training, he is given more challenging cows with which to work.

A cutting saddle is different from most Western saddles. It has a flat seat, which gives the rider a closer feeling to the horse. The seat is longer, allowing the rider to move in the saddle in order to stay with the horse. The horn is taller and narrower to make it easier to grip. It is a truly fantastic experience to ride a cutting horse, to feel the power and control of each calculated movement, all without any direction from the rider.

# SIDESADDLE

According to pictorial records, until the fifteenth century women rode astride with their feet in slipper stirrups. The first variation from riding astride was to sit sideways on a saddle with a step called a *planchette*, suspended by metal or leather straps. It had a pommel or horn to give the rider a handhold. Some women rode sideways behind a man on a single horse. This was termed riding pillion, and was found to be most practical. In the fifteenth century Catherine de Médicis, queen of France, introduced the second horn, or lower pommel, allowing the rider to shift her body more to the front and affording a more secure seat by providing a base of support for the right leg, which hooks over it. Except for the elimination of the footrest, and the substitution of the slipper stirrup, the structure of the sidesaddle remained about the same until the nineteenth century.

Improvements were made for the comfort of the horse; to prevent rubbing on the withers the front of the saddle was cut back, and the frame of the saddle was modified to avoid contact with the animal's spine. Around 1800, the ''balance strap'' was introduced to keep the saddle from shifting on the horse's back without tightening the girth excessively. This strap runs from the back of the saddle, across the girth, to the opposite side of the saddle. At that time women were unable to keep up with men in the field because the two-horned saddles they rode made it difficult for them to stay on a horse in the fast gaits and over fences. It was practically impossible for them to maintain their balance by gripping the horn. In 1830, a French riding master introduced the leaping horn, which wrapped over the left thigh, giving security by helping to hold the rider in the saddle. The slipper stirrup was replaced with the conventional stirrup.

Due to its size and amount of padding, the sidesaddle itself is substantially heavier than an ordinary saddle. There are as many differences in sidesaddles as in regular saddles. It is particularly important that the saddle fit the rider. The sidesaddle is designed for women to sit with both feet on the same side, normally the left, although off-sidesaddles are available. On that side, the saddle has two padded projections placed diagonally, one above the other: the pommel supporting the right leg and the leaping horn for the left thigh, which rests under it with the left foot in the single stirrup iron. The balance strap, which runs from the right rear of the saddle under the horse to the left billet strap, prevents the saddle back from swinging and rubbing the back of the horse.

As time passed sidesaddle attire became more and more sensible. From voluminous skirts and ornate, plumed hats,

Joan in sidesaddle costume

*(Pages 110 and 111)* Joan gallops Leo in a field of spring flowers near the ranch.

styles changed over the years to the same attire worn by men in the twentieth century, with the exception of an apron added that buttoned up the side when the rider was afoot, and unbuttoned just as she mounted the horse. Sidesaddle attire is called a habit and differs from that worn astride chiefly in that an ankle-length skirt is worn. For formal attire in hunter appointments classes, the coat, skirt, and breeches should be dark blue or black, and the headgear a derby or a silk hat with an optional mesh veil fastened around the brim and covering the face. Antique costuming is prevalent in parades, Arabian, and Tennessee Walker classes.

A sidesaddle horse should be of especially good temperament, have comfortable gaits, prominent withers so the saddle won't slip, and a long enough back to accommodate the larger saddle. The horse that responds well to his rider should pose no problem when used with a sidesaddle.

An animal that has never carried a sidesaddle should be allowed time to become acquainted with its different feel. I began by first lunging my horse with the saddle. It is important to check the girth before mounting because it cannot be adjusted from the saddle, and, until you develop a balanced seat, the saddle is more inclined to slip. To mount, you can either be assisted or hop up from a mounting block facing forward and twisted slightly so that you land sitting sideways, then lift your right leg over the pommel. Or, you may mount by using the stirrup, just as on an astride saddle, and then hook your leg over the pommel. To dismount, remove your foot from the stirrup, throw your right leg over the pommel, and slide down with your back to the horse.

The objectives of the sidesaddle rider remain the same as those of the person who rides astride: to direct the horse with a balanced but firm seat in a controlled but relaxed manner. A sidesaddle rider should not lean to one side or the other, or twist her body. Her spine should be straight. She should not lean forward or back. There should be a straight line from the horse's mouth to the rider's elbow, showing a light, steady contact. The left heel should be lower than the left toe, and the rider should avoid putting too much weight on the stirrup. A good sidesaddle rider can post the trot as any other rider would. To offset the absence of a leg on the right side of the horse, a long dressage type of whip is carried to cue the horse in place of the leg. Therefore, a whip is always permissible when riding sidesaddle.

Although I was long an admirer of the sidesaddle, my first attempts to master the art came with the development of the Wild Animal Park horse show. I felt it would add a touch of eloquence and history to the show. Finding a sidesaddle wasn't easy, since most of them are antiques often in poor repair, or imports from the few saddlemakers still producing sidesaddles. I finally tracked down an antique one that was in fairly good shape and checked it carefully for

The elegance and tradition of sidesaddle are especially attractive to Joan.

Here, a sidesaddle can be seen without a skirt covering it.

rotted leather and stitching. With a few repairs it was usable.

For the sidesaddle segment of the park show I chose an Arabian gelding with an elegant look and graceful movement. Neither I nor the other four riders had any experience riding sidesaddle, and I found a sidesaddle rider who agreed to instruct us. She made it look so easy as she cantered effortlessly around the ring.

Although I had ridden many different styles of saddles, on a sidesaddle I felt like a fish out of water at first. I was told to sit as I would on any other saddle, with my body centered and straight and shoulders square, but my body wanted to turn sideways. I had to work to keep my right shoulder back. Once I felt secure at a walk I progressed to the trot, for me the most difficult gait. Experienced at posting, I found rising on the sidesaddle a great challenge because the leaping horn rests against the outside of the left thigh. The horn gives stability at the canter, and the seat is amazingly secure. The only obstacle was picking up the left lead without a leg on the right side of the horse. I had to get used to using a whip instead of my leg. On a few occasions when the horse shied to the left, I thought he was moving out from under me.

Once I became accustomed to riding sidesaddle, I found it very comfortable and secure. It offers a woman the opportunity to feel romantically elegant while carrying on a tradition that is seldom practiced today. Today, the art of riding sidesaddle is finding renewed interest. Happily, it can again be seen in the show ring in hunter, Arabian, Tennessee Walking horse, and pleasure divisions. It is also popular in parades. Queen Elizabeth always rides sidesaddle for the ceremony of Trooping the Colors. Some women still ride to the hounds in this manner in England, Ireland, and parts of the United States.

# DRIVING

Driving is not only one of my favorite equestrian activities, it is the one I can share with others as participants rather than spectators. The young and the old, disabled persons, and even people who have never been on a horse enjoy a carriage or wagon ride.

One morning at breakfast I was looking out the window when I saw a man going down the road in a fine-looking wagon pulled by a pair of horses. Dressed only in my pajamas, I went flying out the door and chased him down the road. The man must have thought he was being pursued by a crazy woman, but I didn't care how I looked. I only wanted him to stop so that I could see his wagon and his horses and ask him how he put the whole thing together. A patient man, he introduced himself as Stan Jones. We talked for some time. Later, he showed me some of the other carriages he had collected and built.

I learned from Stan that training for driving usually starts with ground driving; once a horse is working well at that he is hooked to a training, or breaking, cart. This is a two-wheeled vehicle that is much more maneuverable than are the four-wheeled carts that have a limited turning radius. With a two-wheeled cart, if the horse makes a quick turn to the right or the left, he isn't going to turn a wheel into the side of the vehicle or flip it over. With a practice cart he can actually pivot completely around; he becomes used to being between the shafts, and having to back up, stop, and start while pulling a minimal amount of weight.

As a horse progresses and gains experience, he can then be hooked up to a less maneuverable, four-wheeled vehicle, or be required to pull more weight with, for example, a hitch wagon. Training animals for driving is a gradual process that requires a great deal of patience. Frequently, an inexperienced horse is trained alongside a well-trained animal. Once the green horse has had sufficient ground work and is put into harness, it may be possible to skip the cart phase of training and place him directly into a hitch. By having a calm, trained companion at his side, a green horse accepts being driven more readily. In this way, he is not put into a position that is overly stressful or in which too much is expected of him.

From Stan I purchased a small wagon for a pair of ponies. At the time I only had the pony I had driven as a single cart pony in my horse show at the Wild Animal Park. I found a second pony of the same size and began to train them to drive. When I first hooked them up it was quite amusing,

Joan with her Clydesdale mare Melody.

*(Pages 116 and 117)* Melody pulls a Petaluma show cart.

because one wanted to go lickety-split while the other would sit back in his britching and not do anything. That's what you call a willing pair: one's willing to work and the other's willing to let him do it.

Stan Jones helped me with training my new charges, showing me how to hook them up to the wagon, how to hook up the lines, how to control the one that was going too fast, and how to make the lazy one move by using the whip to drive him up in the harness, so that both ponies pulled together uniformly. When I started to go out on my own I quickly found it was very easy to make mistakes. Hooking up the lines incorrectly meant that instead of having two horses going forward, one wanted to go to the right and the other to the left. The reins are different lengths, since you have one rein from each horse that crosses over the other horse; adjusted properly this keeps them together. If hooked up improperly it can be a problem. Also, if you adjust the traces too long, when the team moves forward the singletree may come off the pole. If they are too short, the vehicle may hit the hind legs of the horses. In the beginning it seemed that I made mistakes each time I went out. Gradually, however, after making countless corrections, I began to develop a feel for driving.

It was a good thing that I started with ponies, because their size and strength were much more controllable than that of horses. Soon, though, my interest grew, as did my desire to drive larger animals. I bought another vehicle from Stan, this time a doctor's buggy. It was beautiful, shiny, and black with burgundy-colored seats, and had a top that rolled up. It was such a pretty vehicle that when Duane and I began making plans to be married, I was determined to drive a horse and carriage for my wedding. My mother thought I was crazy. I remember her saying, ''I will never forgive you if you ruin this wedding.''

So, I set out to train Finally to ground drive. I ground drove him until he was almost, but not quite, ready to be hooked up, when I realized we were running out of time. Because my mother's words were still ringing in my ears and I didn't want to take any chances, I rode Finally down to a Morgan training stable that had driving horses. My problems, however, were not over. At the stable they tightened up the overcheck (a strap that restricts the horse's movement), something I hadn't done. This was too restrictive for an inexperienced animal like Finally. Apart from that, he didn't get along with his new trainer and he started to rear to the point that he would almost go over backward. Less than a week before the wedding when I went to see him, to my dismay the trainer said my horse had become a real problem. It left me no choice but to bring Finally home. Fortunately, Stan came over and the two of us tried to get him ready for the wedding.

I'll never forget the day of our marriage. Although I was worried that Finally would become nervous and give us trouble, I was determined he was going to be in that wedding. I got up early in the morning, hooked Finally to the training cart, and drove him five miles down the road to the dairy and back. I figured, *I'm going to wear this horse down to the point where he can't possibly think about being bad.* We did indeed drive him for the wedding.

From driving a single "light horse," it wasn't long before I set my sights on driving draft horses. I'd seen the Pilegard family with their hitch at the county fair. When I watched them hook up and drive six Percheron draft horses, I thought, *Sometime in my life I have got to try that.* I started by driving Melody and using a farm wagon we had purchased. We had great fun with her, giving hayrides and going on picnics to the valley a few miles from the ranch. Because Melody was so mellow, I began to think that all draft horses were pretty much like her. However, I was in for a bit of a surprise when I hooked up our Percherons Bob and Doc for the first time. They were raring to go. Having been leaders on a six-horse hitch, they really stepped out. When I took the reins for the first time, I think we went a couple of hundred yards before I could slow them down. It seemed they were taking me for a ride instead of vice versa.

In the future I hope to continue from working two draft horses to eventually working four, and maybe someday I'll progress to a six-horse hitch. I did have an opportunity to ride in the hitch wagon with Stan Pilegard when we did a segment on driving for my television series, *The Animal Express.* It's an incredible sensation to sit in the driver's seat and have the control of six two-thousand-pound horses in your hands, directing their every move while the lead horses are more than twenty feet away. The feeling of power is awesome as you sense that through the simple movement of hands, the driver is able to put the horses into position.

Today, the driving of draft horses is primarily a hobby. Though these marvelous animals are making a comeback in the show ring, there are few people who really have a feel for what it takes to put a fine hitch together. I wish I could find an experienced driver with whom I could spend six months studying. Every year the number of older, knowledgeable drivers decreases, leaving behind only a handful of people to pass on their skills. One of the problems in driving is the tremendous expense involved. A fifth-wheel show wagon can cost from ten to twenty thousand dollars, and the harness for each animal may easily exceed the value of the horse. Top show harness runs as much as five thousand dollars per animal. To be able to hook up six horses, at least two and as many as four helpers are needed on the ground. Each horse has to be harnessed separately and

Joan gives her niece Lisa a ride in a pony cart.

*(Pages 120 and 121)* Doc and Joan with a cart ready for the show ring

brought into position on the hitch. Once the first horse is ready to be hooked up, the driver is already on the seat. He is the only person who has control of that horse once it has been put into position.

The expenses of competitive driving do not stop with paying employees and buying horses, harness, and vehicles. If you are going to campaign or show seriously, you must have a van for transporting the wagon, along with six to eight two-thousand-pound horses. All the maneuvers required in the show ring today were derived from the ways in which horses worked in the early 1900s. In most driving exhibitions, moments from history are presented—when teams of horses were used as the primary means of transportation and delivery.

The Anheuser-Busch hitch of eight Clydesdales is one of the major influences in the draft-horse teams of today. Anheuser-Busch supports three hitches that are on the road constantly. The Merrimack, New Hampshire, team covers the East Coast; the St. Louis team covers the Midwest; and the Warm Springs Ranch team, based at Romoland, California, is used on the West Coast. Anheuser-Busch has been breeding Clydesdales for more than fifty years, and the horses became its symbol on April 7, 1933. These horses are exhibited with great style in fairs, rodeos, parades, and major events all over the country. Most people simply can't afford to ship, show, and support their horses in the grand manner that the Busch people do. The West Coast hitch has three vans, forty feet in length, which haul the eight horses used to pull the wagon, plus two back-up animals. Busch flies its farrier anyplace in the country to shoe its hitch horses, wherever he might be needed. The Busch people have a closed-circuit camera in the temperature-controlled vans so that they can watch the horses in the trailers while traveling. One van is used for transporting the harness and the wagon, the second van holds six horses, and the third one carries four horses and portable stalls, just in case they need them. Their harnesses alone cost more than forty thousand dollars per team. They have spectacular fifth-wheel wagons, with brass appointments and some of the best drivers in the country. Each team has a crew of six men, including two people whose primary assignment is to clean harness.

We were fortunate that the Anheuser-Busch people recently stayed with us and stabled their horses at our ranch during one of their exhibitions in San Diego. It was a spectacular sight to watch so many of these immense, beautifully conditioned horses being unloaded at the same time, and people came to the ranch from all over the county to see them. A tremendous amount of time was spent every day washing the horses' feathers—their long, white lower-leg hairs—with Castile soap. The feathers were scrubbed and combed so that when the eight horses trotted down the road, the snow-white feathers flowed with their movement to give them an even more spectacular appearance. In order to be

able to wash the horses daily, the Anheuser-Busch crew carry with them a small hot-water heater. Not a penny is spared on making this horse hitch as beautiful as possible.

The morning before their exhibition the horses were all exercised by being ridden bareback or with bareback pads. I was fortunate enough to be able to ride one of them. I had ridden Melody, who has won many riding classes at the Los Angeles County Fair, but the Budweiser horse I rode was so broad, I could hardly keep my legs wrapped around his sides. He had so much power it was really a challenge to stay on his back. While one horse is ridden, one or two additional animals are exercised by being ponied on either side of the mounted horse. I can barely express the joy I felt while watching those huge horses ridden around the ring by men who were dwarfed by their size.

Finally hitched to a doctor's wagon with a llama tied behind

I think that the Budweiser hitch causes most people to believe that all draft horses are eighteen to twenty hands tall, which is not really the case. The Anheuser-Busch Clydesdales are extremely large for the breed—several of them, at the withers, towered above me. I would guess that they stand a good nineteen hands (a hand being four inches), which is well over six feet at the withers. It is a tremendous responsibility to drive a team of these immense, powerful animals in a parade, or any other place where there are hundreds of spectators, many of them children, on foot.

When a horse is hooked up in harness to a cart or a driving vehicle, he must accept a certain amount of restraint that is placed on him. If he does not accept this restraint, a potentially dangerous situation is created. Occasionally, an ac-

cident will occur when a horse panics, at which time he has the power to overturn the vehicle, jump up over the shafts, or tear up the harness. A horse that is selected for driving must have an even temperament and be controllable. Only once have I seen a runaway team—a pair of hackneys—and it was terrifying to see them running as fast as they could while literally throwing the carriage behind them every which way. One of the drivers went flying off and landed on his back, while the other was trying to do the best he could to get the panicked animals under control. Unfortunately, he was unable to do so before they ran through a large crowd of people at a fairground. When you see such runaway horses and the potential danger they create, it really gives you a respect for reinsmanship and good training.

# PLEASURE

My own experiences with horses began as a pleasurable pastime. I remember sitting on a riding-school horse with my arms wrapped around its neck in sheer ecstasy. I thought any horse was beautiful and I was totally content just to be around them. Every ride was an experience of joy, companionship, and discovery. There was so much to learn, and the world somehow looked different from atop a horse. It was what I lived for. As my abilities expanded, I became more demanding of my skills and those of my horse. I seemed driven with an insatiable desire to learn. I have competed in many phases of horsemanship, but somehow, as time has passed, I have come to realize that as much as I enjoy the competition, the real reason I have my horses is the pleasure I derive from them, not how many blue ribbons they win. I love to walk through the barn, even when I get home late at night. After a long day at work, seeing my horses makes it all worthwhile. The soft nickers of acknowledgment, the smell of fresh bedding, the feel of the warm soft muzzles and sleek coats are a more than adequate reward for all the work and worry and expense.

The American Horse Council reports there are approximately three and one half million people in the United States who own the estimated nine million horses in this country, of which only 20 percent are owned for commercial or agricultural uses. Horse owners spend more than seven billion dollars annually on feed, equipment, drugs, services, and related items. Six billion dollars is invested in horses and related assets, two and one half billion dollars in land and buildings. Interestingly enough, horseracing is America's number one spectator sport, producing a revenue of seven hundred million dollars.

Americans have more leisure time and more money than ever before. The pressures of city life drive many people into the country on weekends and holidays, where some people find it more convenient to buy and maintain horses of their own rather than renting or leasing them. Yet, the countryside for horse keeping is becoming less available and more expensive. Why would someone spend so much, drive so far, and work so hard for something that is not a

With a pack horse behind, Joan pauses with her Quarter Horse Gray Ray to enjoy a view of the valley.

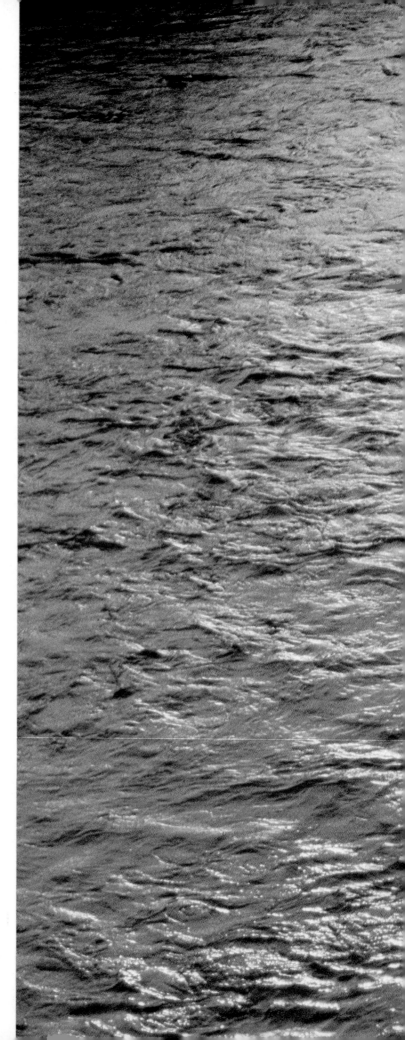

necessity? Pleasure! Pleasure riding can mean many different things to different people. To a person in New York, it may mean a Sunday ride in Central Park. To a rider in the western United States, pleasure riding may mean riding out with a pack mule to spend days camping in the wilderness.

On my days off there isn't anything quite like a ride through the mountains, the desert, or the beach, the feeling of discovery, of being a part of nature with the companionship of another creature. There is an awakening of the senses that somehow become dulled with the pressures of daily life. It gives me time to think, a peaceful moment with undemanding companionship. Although I see deer daily in the zoo, to come upon a doe and fawn in the woods, and to watch them freeze then dash away is special. To cross a gurgling stream, crunch through the snow, or play in the surf on horseback is to experience life at its best. Some of my greatest pleasures in life have been with my horses.

Pleasure riding is one of Joan's favorite equestrian activities.

# ACKNOWLEDGMENTS

Some of Joan's twenty-five horses appear with many of the people who kindly helped with this book.

*M*y sincere thanks go to the following friends who gave of their time and expertise in the completion of this project. Torrey Pillsbury spent hours transcribing tapes and assisting in research. Her experience with horses was invaluable as she backed me up in preparing each of the many horses we photographed. Edith Adams was always ready to lend a hand in any way. From cleaning horses, harness, and carriages to running for food or film, she kept things going when we needed an extra hand. Hazel True designed and made my costumes and gave her support to keep the ranch running smoothly. Cheryl Lenz spent much of her spare time helping with the project. Jerry Lucas and Chad Usherwood, who train cutting horses on the ranch, gave their time and expertise, and Charlie Comfort lent his wonderful horse, Bar De Bye. Christy Anderson, who was my first instructor, shared his understanding of horses with me, and I am grateful to him for many years of pleasure. If it were not for my parents, Vernon and Shirley Embery, who made hundreds of trips to the stables with me, I might never have gone on to live my dream.

Some of the other people who gave generously of their time were: Eddie Brugman, Janet and Dannie Cole, Carrie Drake, Valerie Escalera, Bill Ivy, Charlotte Kneeland, Joan Langdon, Dr. Terry Paik, Holly Pillsbury, Oliver Ryder, Jill Santillan, Fred Schmidt, Chris Sibel, Randy Steffan, Laura Tietz, and Francisco Magana Torres.

—JOAN EMBERY

Apart from the people on Joan's list, who have my deepest appreciation, I would especially like to thank my great friend and assistant Joe Saccoman. The San Diego Zoo and the San Diego Wild Animal Park provided valuable assistance, and I would especially like to thank Rich Massena and Martha Baker. For believing in this project and offering their continuing encouragement I thank my agent, Gloria Loomis; and at William Morrow, Howard Cady, Larry Hughes, Sherry Arden, Al Marchioni, Lela Rolontz, John Ball, Bernard Schleifer, and Randee Marullo. Mary Talley Willmont provided valuable help while I was doing the design, as did Nancy Ridley. I thank Ron and Gale Vavra for taking care of me during my work on this book.

—ROBERT VAVRA